MOTHERS, MURDERS, & MOTIVATION

A Journey Through the Mind and Heart of a Prosecutor

JARRETT FERENTINO

WITH RON LIEBACK

A POST HILL PRESS BOOK
ISBN: 979-8-89565-462-0
ISBN (eBook): 979-8-89565-463-7

Mothers, Murders, and Motivation:
A Journey Through the Mind and Heart of a Prosecutor

Cover design by Jim Villaflores

This is a work of nonfiction. All people, locations, events, and situations are portrayed to the best of the author's memory and knowledge. Although adequate research was undergone concerning criminal cases, real-life people and perceptions, and authentic situations and incidents, the author and publisher do not assume and hereby disclaim any liability concerning any legal or criminal details present in this book.

Post Hill Press
New York • Nashville
posthillpress.com

Published in the United States of America
1 2 3 4 5 6 7 8 9 10

This book is dedicated to the women who shaped my heart and the children who gave it purpose.

To my mother, Rose, the first example of strength, sacrifice, and unconditional love I ever knew. Every value that guided me through the darkest courtrooms and the hardest cases began with you and was a tribute to you.

To my wife, Nicole, an extraordinary wife and mother whose grace, patience, and love carried our family while I chased justice and truth. You bore more than your share so that I could do this work, and I will forever be grateful.

And to my children, Dominick and Victoria, my greatest inspiration. You sacrificed time with Daddy so I could stand for others who had no voice. Every page that follows exists because I wanted to build something worthy of you.

Everything in this book—and everything I strive to be—begins and ends with you.

—Jarrett Ferentino

To Jarrett Ferentino, thank you for your trust and for allowing me to help carry a story rooted in truth, loss, and motivation.

To Jay Valenti, whose call set this project in motion. Our miles on the road and endless conversations along the way continue to guide me.

And to my wife, Pam, and my son, Enzo, thank you for being my foundation. Your support carries me through the chaos, the creativity, and the quiet moments in between.

—Ron Lieback

Contents

BOOK 3 - THE BABY WHO COULD HAVE BEEN PRESIDENT

Commonwealth v. Tiffany Simmons and Alan Leitzel

BOOK 4 - THE MOVIE STAR MURDERER

Commonwealth v. Hugo Selenski

BOOK 5 - THE SPRING BREAK MURDER

South Carolina v. Raymond Moody

Foreword by Nancy Grace

NO ONE EVER SAID IT would be easy; in fact, being a felony prosecutor is tough. It takes all your time, all your energy, and all your heart…that is, if you do it right. Jarrett Ferentino did it right.

If you are OK with violent felons walking free on light sentences and sweetheart plea deals, the job is a cake walk. If, however, you take on each case with a crime victim and what is best for her or him in mind, it's anything but easy. Also, you get a government salary no matter how hard you work, and overtime pay doesn't exist.

If you do it right, you must be a believer…a believer in right and wrong and that it is your duty to seek verdicts that speak the truth, no matter what. You serve Lady Justice.

Jarrett has spent the majority of his legal career doing just that; day after day, week after week, year after year, seeking justice. The cases he investigated and prosecuted have become the story of his life for those years…ingrained in who he is.

Growing up in coal country after his dad passed away, he watched his mother sacrifice everything to support her boys and wage her own battle to support them in a male-dominated field. Not only did she compete, she won. She met and surpassed her male counterparts in one of the largest corporations in the world, Prudential. A wife and a mom left with a briefcase and a lot of heart, resulting in her family learning life lessons about grit and determination.

That grit and determination Jarrett saw in his mother, Rose, transformed him into the trial lawyer he is today. In his amazing book, he details not only the stories, but the people he met along the way. The stories of mothers he fought for in court, the stories and the people that touched his life.

Jarrett Ferentino, trial lawyer, advocate, TV star...friend. I hope you enjoy taking this journey with him in *Mothers, Murders, and Motivation.*

Nancy A. Grace
Host, *Crime Stories*
Author, *Objection*!
Eleventh Victim
Death on the D-List
Murder in the Courthouse
Don't Be A Victim
What Happened to Ellen?

INTRODUCTION

UNIVERSITY OF FERENTINO

"There are winds of destiny that blow when we least expect them. Sometimes they gust with the fury of a hurricane, sometimes they barely fan one's cheek. But the winds cannot be denied, bringing as they often do a future that is impossible to ignore."

—Nicholas Sparks, *Message in a Bottle*

IN 1977, MY FATHER, GARY Ferentino, a postman, and my mother, Rose, a homemaker, had two sons, Maurice and Jude. As our family grew, they left their rental in Old Forge, Pennsylvania, and built a small ranch home about ten minutes away in Pittston, tucked beneath the shadow of the culm bank mountains, the black hills reminiscent of the coal industry boom in that area.

My grandmother, Marion Ferentino, bought the lot across the street so she could be near her only son and grandsons. Life seemed to be moving forward. But during a doctor's visit, my parents got a surprise. Not only was my mom pregnant again, but she was carrying twins.

Jason and I were born on January 6, 1978.

Our house was fun, loud, chaotic, and full of love, with four Italian boys under the age of five. My dad worked nights and tried to sleep during the day while we raised hell.

We were altar boys, attended Catholic school, and played Little League (not well) on the field behind our home. We were that last generation of kids who played outside and rode bikes with neighborhood buddies until the streetlights came on.

On March 17, 1983, my father won $2,500 playing the lottery. In August, he used his winnings and surprised us with a trip to California to visit my uncle and go to Disneyland. That trip lives forever in my memory. I sat beside my dad on the plane. We visited family and went to Disneyland and Knott's Berry Farm.

There's a picture in my law office from that trip, of our whole family crammed into an antique car with the world ahead of us. Sadly, it's the last photo of all of us together.

That was the beginning of the end, and our luck was about to run out.

My dad, who had been in incredible shape and a runner, had been losing weight and suffering from back pain. I remember him squirming in pain during the flight home. A few days later, he went to the doctor. They found a tumor the size of a grapefruit. The cancer was aggressive. He was given three months to live. He fought for a year and a half.

Our world collapsed.

My mother stayed at his bedside through it all: feeding tubes, bone marrow transplants, the haze of morphine. She contracted a staph infection from being at the hospital so much and nearly died herself. That Christmas, in 1984, both my parents were in separate hospital rooms. Thankfully, my mother survived and became stronger.

My brothers and I were forced to grow up fast.

We were cared for by our grandmothers, Grammy and Nana, while we watched our family unravel.

On February 24, 1985, we were called to the hospital. My dad didn't look like the man I remembered. I cried because I didn't recognize the bald, yellowish man who remained. My father told my mother, "If one of us has to go, I'm glad it's me because you're stronger." He then asked her to promise him two things: never hit us, and make sure we received an education.

My father died that night. And as for Mom, she kept both promises.

I never really had the chance to know my father. Part of him lives on with my brothers and me. Anyone who ever knew him always said he was a gentleman and a good man. I do have memories of his smile, affinity for running, and love for all of us. They say a boy is never truly a man until he buries his father. This was one of the most defining moments of my life, maybe even the most defining moment.

My mother's life was in shambles. My father's war on cancer had drained our finances, and she was left to raise us.

My mother was left broke and widowed, with four young sons. She had grown up poor and been raised by Grammy, Ida Bartoli, one of the strongest women I've ever known. She had known hard times and had witnessed the power of her own strong mother.

Grammy had cleaned houses to make ends meet and would regularly go without food to feed her two children. She was an uneducated child of poor Italian immigrants. Like most of that generation of women in my local town, she also worked in a dress factory and joined the local International Ladies Garment Workers Union (ILGWU). She worked endlessly, and her hands became arthritic and stiff as she grew older.

My mother had that same fire and love for her children. She inherited my grandmother's relentless work ethic and quiet strength. She had been raising four boys while watching her husband fade away before her eyes. And now, with a house full of children and no income, she had to step into the workforce, something she hadn't prepared for but was absolutely ready to conquer.

A childhood friend had once sold her a life insurance policy from Prudential. After my father passed, that friend delivered the check and left her with more than just a payout—he left her with an opportunity. He told her that Prudential was always looking for motivated people. He looked her in the eye and said he thought she'd be great at it.

A few weeks later, she joined the company. She hung up her apron, picked up a briefcase, and walked straight into the lion's den of an industry dominated by men. She had never been in sales before, but she attacked it like a woman who had no choice but to win. And win she did.

She worked sixty, sometimes seventy, hours a week. Tirelessly. She learned everything she could. I'd watch her talk to everyone we met—strangers, neighbors, waiters, parents at school events—about their insurance needs. She didn't use gimmicks or manipulation. She listened, she cared, and she made you believe in the value of what she was offering.

She had that kind of presence.

My mother quickly rose through the ranks. There was no stopping her. She wasn't just selling policies; she was dominating the business. She was dignified, professional, unshakably driven. She made her mark and began earning serious money.

My mother could sell ice to the Eskimos, and they'd come back the next day for more.

Today, many parents never miss a game or a school event. And that's a beautiful thing. But I remember looking out into the stands during games and seeing empty seats where my mom and dad should have been. And you know what? It never bothered me. Not once.

Because I knew where my mom was. She was out there hustling. Building something better. Keeping a promise.

She was doing what she had to do so her four boys could go further than she ever had.

And she did it. She made good on that promise to my father, every single bit of it. She rose all the way to become the head of her Prudential office, and then of the entire region. She retired at the top of her game, just like I'd known she would.

As the years passed, my beautiful mother began to go out socially.

She met a man named Charles Grimes. Now, let's stop right there. It takes a special kind of man to ask a widow with four Italian boys on a date. That's no casual commitment. That's a declaration of courage. But Charlie? He didn't flinch.

On their very first date, my mom brought him straight to our house. No secrets, no surprises. She told him plainly, "You need to meet the boys. This is who I am, and this is what you're getting involved with."

I remember meeting Charlie. I liked him right away. He was calm and kind and never tried too hard. He wasn't there to replace anyone; he was a gentleman, quietly, the way good men do.

They dated for a while, and eventually, when I was twelve years old, they were married.

Despite her demanding job, my mom always made sure she was home for supper with us. She would make sure our family was together. My grandmothers were a tremendous help. Charlie was an amazing support to her as well. We rebuilt our family in the wake of my father's death. We moved forward together.

My mother is appropriately named Rose. A rose is a beautiful flower, but it has thorns to protect it from being eaten by predators. A rose also uses its thorns to grow past the rocks and weeds and into the sunshine where it can grow and flourish. That's my mother.

Looking back, I could never repay my mother for the sacrifices she made, for what she endured, and for how hard she fought for us. I've thought about it a thousand times. But if I ever offered to try to repay her, she'd shut it down fast.

Instead, she gave me something else.

She said, "You're going to meet people in life, especially mothers, who are struggling. Help them. That's how you can thank me."

And I never forgot that.

I kept moving forward—my brothers and I all did. We went to elementary school at St. Mary's Assumption, a Catholic school, where I struggled.

The school grouped students into smaller categories: the "ones" were the smart, advanced kids. The "twos" were the average learners. And then there were the "threes." I landed in the "threes."

That label stuck, even if the system was cruel and outdated. "Three" meant trouble. "Three" meant behavioral issues. "Three" back then meant "challenged."

But I wasn't trouble or challenged, I was distracted and couldn't focus.

Looking back, I know I likely had undiagnosed attention deficit disorder. I couldn't sit still. I couldn't hold a thought. I would zone out through entire lessons, then wake up when the bell rang having heard nothing.

My notebooks weren't filled with notes. They were filled with stories. Little sketches. Imaginings of worlds far from the one I was sitting in. I created adventures at the bottom of the page while my teachers droned on above me.

I wasn't wired like the other kids. We would play sports in the neighborhood or organized baseball and basketball. I had zero confidence in my academics and even less in my athletic abilities. I was always the last person picked for a team, if I was picked at all. I would rarely play in any game and would sit on the bench even in practice. Somehow, I was still hungry to prove something. I always felt like an underdog but believed that I had something to offer the world.

As a kid, I was obsessed with Al Pacino and Rocky Balboa. I'd stand in the mirror and deliver full monologues from *Scent of a Woman* and *...And Justice for All,* channeling Pacino's fury, timing, and fire. And Rocky? He wasn't just a boxer. He was the ultimate underdog, the guy who wasn't supposed to win but did anyway because he never gave up.

Even now, after all these years, I still see myself, and my law cases, that same way.

My brother Jason and I went on to attend Seton Catholic, a small high school tucked into Pittston, Pennsylvania. I loved that place. Every day felt like a gift.

By sophomore year, I ran for student body president and won. The school was partially staffed by sisters of the Immaculate Heart of Mary (IHM), who taught us more than math and writing; they taught us mercy. Discipline wrapped in compassion. The school was a place where I finally felt understood.

Those years gave me something else, too: lifelong friendships. My closest friends—Michael Lombardo and Matt Golden—stood by me from that small high school all the way through college and law school. We didn't just grow up together; we built lives side by side.

But my education wasn't limited to what I learned in actual school. I received an education outside of the classroom as well.

Across the street from our house lived my Nana and her brother, my great-uncle Godfrey. He had contracted polio in the 1930s and could no longer walk without crutches. Steel braces supported his legs. He shuffled. He leaned. But he never quit.

Godfrey became like a grandfather to me. We were a pair. When I was younger, we'd wax his car, plant flowers, and sit in silence, watching the world go by from the attached garage. He was a quiet man, full of pride, and very alone. But I never saw our time together as a chore. He needed someone, and I showed up. As a kid in the "threes" and regularly on the bench, it was nice to have someone who valued me.

As the years passed, Godfrey's body began to fail. He fell more often. Bursitis attacked his elbows. He lost strength. Eventually, he couldn't get out of bed, his car, or even the bathroom by himself. He and I kept that reality hidden from the rest of the family—he was terrified of being sent to a nursing home.

So, I changed my schedule.

I was there in the morning. After school. At night. I did what needed to be done—because he needed me. I would assist him in getting to his feet or into a wheelchair. He was able to take it from there. He just needed that lifting up in those moments.

It wasn't easy.

There were nights when he cried, begging to die. Nights when he told me he was going to end it. And I was just a kid, scrambling for words, trying to find something to hold him here. To make it better. To make it matter. I would say, "Don't say that. Who am I going to hang out with?" I would count the good things in his life and say, "You're being too negative." We would make it through one day at a time.

Helping Godfrey was my first real taste of advocacy, of standing up for someone who couldn't do it themselves. It taught me that life is brutal. Unfair. Unforgiving. But it also showed me what quiet strength looks like. I wanted to find a way to fight for people like him in my life.

He eventually passed away while I was in college. I was there when he passed. But I still talk to him. Still call on him. I feel him with me, especially in the hard moments.

And in my law office, high on a bookshelf, sits his cap. A daily reminder that no matter what fight I'm in, no matter how dark or difficult the road gets, it's nothing compared to what Godfrey faced with grace, every single day.

The philosopher Søren Kierkegaard said that our personal experiences are the only way to truly understand our existence. For me, that understanding came while caring for my uncle. When you sit face-to-face with desperation—real, raw, soul-wrecking desperation—it either breaks you or builds something inside you. For me, it lit a fire.

I knew I had to keep it together.

Godfrey needed me to be steady when everything in him was falling apart. I had to be calm in the chaos, a rock in the storm. I'd whisper it to myself all the time: "Be strong."

Not for me, but for him.

I never let him see pity in my eyes. I never complained, even when I was exhausted. He relied on me to show up and be solid. So, I did, and I was. Because anything less would have betrayed our bond.

Looking back, I see that he was the first person I ever fought for. A victim of life's circumstances and cruelty. A man who still woke up and tried, even when the world gave him no reason to.

And in a very real, very profound way, he shaped me.

He taught me how to stay composed when everything is falling apart. He gave me a blueprint for resilience. I started to understand something that no report card or trophy ever could show me: that what I lacked in academics or athletics didn't matter compared with what I could shoulder in real life.

Life doesn't care who you want to be.

It demands who you must become.

A good son. A strong man. A faithful friend. A protector. That became my path. And only years later did I understand something deeper: while I thought I was lifting him up, the truth is, he was lifting me.

• • •

My mother, as I said, made good on her promise to my father.

She never raised a hand to us, even when we probably deserved it, and she found a way to educate all four of her boys.

My oldest brother, Maurice, became a federal agent and has since retired with honor. He is now a security expert for a national bank. Jude and Jason found their path in the pharmaceutical world, building stable, meaningful, and rewarding careers. They are also incredible fathers and sons.

I earned my bachelor's degree from the McGowan School of Business at King's College in Wilkes-Barre, then kept going, graduating from the Penn State Dickinson School of Law in Carlisle in 2003.

In Northeast Pennsylvania, we are a news town. We have two daily newspapers and two local news stations. Throughout my childhood the Luzerne County Courthouse was a castle from which so much news flowed. I would read the newspaper every day and was intrigued by the homicide cases over the years. I was curious about the defendants and followed the attorneys and key players in the media over the years. I was intrigued by these cases and people. I was attracted to the prosecution side of things. So when the time came, I became a prosecutor—a job that allowed me, sometimes on the same day, to drive a stake through the heart of a predator and begin to help mend the soul of a survivor. That kind of work doesn't just change lives; it transforms yours.

But I had no interest in being just another prosecutor. I wasn't going to stand in front of a jury and give the textbook opening or the dry, rehearsed closing. I wasn't going to walk the walk or talk the talk of what a prosecutor was supposed to be.

I had a different plan.

I remember being in prosecutor school when an instructor said, "'High profile' is a bad word. We don't want high-profile cases."

I sat there thinking, *Really? The pay sucks. The workload is crushing. The stress eats you alive. And now you're telling me we're supposed to avoid the biggest challenges? No Super Bowls—just regular games forever?*

That didn't sit right with me. I wanted the big fights. I wanted cases that went beyond the courthouse walls. I wasn't doing this to whisper in the shadows. I had come to be a voice.

A voice for people like my mother.

A voice for people like my uncle.

And I wasn't going to do it quietly. No more sitting on the bench.

This is my story.

Book 1

THE FAIR QUEEN MURDER

Commonwealth v. Joseph Gacha

"It is important to fight and fight again, and keep fighting, for only then can evil be kept at bay though never quite eradicated."

—J. K. Rowling, *Harry Potter and the Half-Blood Prince*

CHAPTER 1

THE PINK PURSE

MAY 29, 2004. IT WAS a sunny, warm afternoon, one of those deceptively serene spring days in Northeastern Pennsylvania when you'd never expect horror to reveal itself.

Thomas Kurisky was cutting grass on Rear Street in Edwardsville, his mower humming across the yard. It was a chore like any other weekend chore.

As was his routine, he dumped his first bag of clippings in a small wooded area across from his house, near the railroad tracks that ran parallel to the property. That day, he noticed a pink purse and some clothing scattered in the brush. Assuming it was discarded trash, something he had seen there before, he paid little attention.

But when he returned with the second bag, something caught his eye. Inside the pink purse, he saw what looked like a check. Curious, he reached in and pulled it out. It was an IRS check made out to Carrie Martin for sixty-five dollars. The purse, he realized, appeared to have blood on it.

The name jolted him. He'd heard it in the news.

His heart began to race. Without hesitation, Kurisky ran back inside his house and called 911.

Within minutes, the Pennsylvania State Police and local authorities converged and quickly secured the area. The street was closed, and evidence collection teams launched a grid search of the surrounding woods.

Along with the bloodstained purse, police recovered a blue denim men's button-down shirt, a pair of tan-and-brown men's cargo shorts, and a white turtleneck sweater.

Every item was marked with blood stains or spatter.

CHAPTER 2

CARRIE AND JIMMY

CARRIE LYNN MARTIN WAS BORN on June 11, 1983. The only child of Thomas Martin and Wendy Cadwalader, she was raised in a world filled with animals, hard work, and close family ties.

Carrie was beautiful and funny, too. But she was more than that. Tough. Loyal. She stood up for other students who were picked on and never backed down from a fight. She was the kind of girl who'd knock you on your ass if you messed with someone she loved.

She grew up around horses and hayfields. Not the soft kind of country life romanticized in storybooks, but the real kind. She could clean a stable before most people woke up and look flawless doing it. She became a Pennsylvania state champion draft horse driver.

Then, in 2003, she earned the title of Luzerne County Fair Queen. It wasn't just a crown; it was recognition. People knew her. They admired her.

She had a future.

In spring 2024, Carrie was dating Jimmy Burge, her high school sweetheart. She had begun dating Jimmy when they were just seventeen and they were both students at West Side Technical

School. Both of them had come from that hardworking, blue-collar world where pride came from sweat and calluses.

They graduated in 2003 and eventually moved in together, settling into Jimmy's grandmother's house on Howard Street in Larksville. They spent most of their time in a converted garage behind the house, known affectionately as "the Music Room."

It was detached from the main home and filled with mismatched furniture—a few couches, a coffee table, a TV, and a mattress on the floor. It looked like a modest college apartment. Jimmy's father and grandmother lived inside the main house.

The Music Room held history.

It was where Jimmy's grandfather, a bluegrass musician with the Back Mountain Stream Band, had once played with his bandmates. As a child, Jimmy would sit beside him, learning the mandolin and falling in love with music.

Jimmy had followed in his grandfather's footsteps. He spent hours in that garage playing guitar and writing songs. Over time, the Music Room became a gathering place—for him, for Carrie, for their friends. It was theirs.

On May 27, 2004, Jimmy finished his overnight shift at Trion Industries, where he had just started working as a packer. His hours were 11 p.m. to 7 a.m.

He drove home, showered, and made his way out to the Music Room. Carrie was asleep on the mattress.

Around 8 a.m., Jimmy gently woke her up. She was attending the Academy of Creative Hair Design and had class that morning. She dreamed of owning a hair-and-nail salon one day.

Carrie awoke and went into the main house to shower and get ready for school. Her Jeep was at her mother's house and wasn't running right, so Jimmy drove her. He dropped her off at beauty school around 9 a.m., then went back home to get some sleep.

He stayed in the Music Room, sleeping until about 6 p.m.

Carrie's mom, Wendy, was picking her up from school that evening and planned to take her back to her Jeep. Carrie also had a shift that night at her part-time job at You've Got Nails, a salon in Kingston Township.

Around 7 p.m., Carrie called Jimmy. Her Jeep still wasn't working, and she needed a ride. Jimmy picked her up. On the way home, they stopped at the McDonald's drive-through in Kingston Township.

They returned to the Music Room, ate, and spent more time together. They relaxed, watched TV, and played video games—normal things—before Jimmy had to head to work. Around 10:30 p.m., he got ready, went into the main house, and said goodnight to his father and grandmother.

Jimmy's shift, as noted above, started at 11 p.m. Around 1 a.m., during his break, he called Carrie—something he always did. She didn't answer. He called again. Still no answer.

That wasn't like her.

Worried, Jimmy called his grandmother. He asked if she could check on Carrie. She did. A short time later, she called him back.

She lied and said, "She's sleeping."

But Carrie wasn't sleeping. What Jimmy's grandmother had seen was not sleep—it was death.

In shock, she called 911.

CHAPTER 3

DO NOT CROSS

THE CALL FROM DISTRICT ATTORNEY Dave Lupas woke me up in the dead of night. I'd been working in the DA's office for only a mere eight weeks, but I was hungry to be on a case.

Lupas said there'd been a murder in Larksville, and he wanted me to be on this case: "Get over there, OK?"

I threw on clothes and hit the road. When I arrived, the scene was chaotic: crime scene tape, flashing lights, a crowd, and a large presence of law enforcement in the rear driveway near the home's detached garage.

Those around the crime scene all had expressions that told me this wasn't routine. You could smell it in the air: blood, despair, the heaviness of something wrong.

I ducked under the tape, and an officer moved to stop me. I was a new assistant district attorney, an unknown face to the officers at the time. I pulled out my badge, saying, "I'm with the District Attorney's Office." That was the first and last time I went unrecognized at a crime scene.

My heart was racing, but I was calm. I signed the crime scene log. I crossed under that infamous "do not cross" yellow tape, which changed me forever.

I immediately noticed the look on some of the young officers' faces. Their eyes were wide. Whatever was in that garage had terrified them.

I remember the deputy coroner, Bill Lisman. I approached Bill and joined a conversation about what was inside the garage. We were standing just beyond the door into the garage.

I was told that a young woman had been murdered. The crime appeared deeply personal. She had been stabbed repeatedly. It was a bloody scene.

I had to walk through that door into the garage, and I knew that once I did, there would be no turning back.

I entered the Music Room, and there was Carrie. Partially covered. Lifeless. Her wounds were so extensive that it took every ounce of focus for me not to be overwhelmed.

She had been stabbed dozens of times. The brutality was personal. Whoever did this didn't just want her gone—they wanted her erased.

Never before had I felt such shock overwhelm every inch of my body. It did more than cause hairs to stand up on the back of my neck; it was downright nauseating. I couldn't believe a human being could do that to another human being. If I hadn't known better, I would have thought she had been mauled by a bear.

Her head looked like it was nearly severed. The depth of the wounds across her body was staggering, as was the amount of blood splattered and pooled everywhere.

And my very next thought? I swore then to myself, standing in that carnage, that I would prosecute whoever had done this. I was going to get them and bring them to justice for this poor girl, who I later learned was only twenty years old. Twenty!

I walked into the Music Room as a naive and hungry twenty-six-year-old man, and I walked out as a prosecutor.

The room itself, as I mentioned earlier, looked like a college apartment. Grateful Dead posters, music paraphernalia, and a blue acoustic guitar. The door had "Jimmy and Carrie" and "The Music Room" painted on it. It looked like a happy place where kids hung out.

But the walls were now painted in Carrie's blood.

The mattress was soaked, and pools of blood surrounded her young body. She had a long T-shirt on, and her lower half was bare and partially covered by a pillow that was caked in blood. The T-shirt had slash and stab marks on it. It was ripped and bunched up on her back, clearly showing signs of struggle.

My mind was racing. Was this a drug deal gone bad? Was this the work of a psychotic serial killer? What actually happened here?

No one really knew anything.

Out of the corner of my eye, I saw an older woman in shock, the grandmother of Carrie's boyfriend, Jimmy Burge. She owned the home and this garage space, where we learned Jimmy had been living with Carrie.

Jim Burge Sr. was outside speaking with investigators.

I was then introduced to State Trooper Lisa Brogan and recognized County Detective Gary Sworen from the District Attorney's Office. Lisa was a well-known state trooper assigned to the criminal investigative unit, but this was her first homicide case as a lead. She was the only female trooper in that unit, and I immediately respected her because of that; my mother's influence immediately surfaced.

Lisa briefed me on Carrie's background as it was reported by Jim Burge Sr., and I was told she had been close with her mother. Had her mother found out yet? And should a mother even see such a horrific scene? That soft boy inside me began to emerge, which hardened the prosecutor on the outside.

This emotion is one thing that followed me throughout my twenty years in the District Attorney's Office. And it still does today; although I'm no longer prosecuting, I still feel this when discussing other cases as a legal analyst.

Detective Gary Sworen and I immediately became friends. He turned out to be one of the most composed people I have ever worked with. He was a tremendous detective and handled some of the biggest cases in Luzerne County history.

Gary prefaced everything with, "Here's what we're doing." He then filled me in quickly on what was occurring. He recognized that I was new and needed to learn. He was patient with me from the outset and was willing to teach me. I realized that I had much to learn from him and many on the scene.

The first suspect was obviously Jimmy, the boyfriend. Statistically, that's how it usually goes. Investigators had already sent a detective and a state trooper to Jimmy's place of employment, Trion Industries.

A command post was set up at the Pennsylvania State Police barracks in the borough of Wyoming. I left the scene and joined the investigators in the crime room. I would spend countless days and nights in that building and room over the course of my career.

I knew Jimmy was going to be brought in, and I sat in as investigators started to put the case together.

Luzerne County detective Larry Fabian and trooper Steve "Turk" Turinski drove to Trion Industries in Plains. They asked to speak with Jimmy Burge.

Jimmy's manager, unaware of the investigation's true purpose, assumed the visit was about a series of recent thefts from the company dumpster. He walked over to Jimmy and told him the police were there to see him. Jimmy looked confused.

The manager added, "It's probably about the dumpster stuff."

Jimmy stepped outside. He saw Fabian and Turk waiting. Turk approached first.

"Are you Jimmy Burge?" he asked.

Jimmy replied, "Yes."

"Is Carrie Martin your girlfriend?"

Jimmy again said yes.

Turk didn't ease into it. "She was murdered."

Jimmy turned white. He went into shock and almost passed out.

Turk had been deliberately blunt. At that point, Jimmy was a likely suspect, and Turk wanted to observe his reaction. Turk later said Jimmy's reaction appeared to be genuine shock.

They brought Jimmy to the state police barracks in Wyoming and pressed him. What did he know? Had he hurt Carrie? Did he know anyone who might have? Was he dealing drugs?

Jimmy was scared, but he told them the truth. He couldn't think of anyone who would have wanted to hurt Carrie. Or him.

Jimmy didn't flinch. His shock was real. His pain was raw. Suspicion of him waned pretty quickly.

That meant we had to go wider.

Lieutenant Frank Hacken from the state police wrote up a to-do list on an easel and started assigning tasks. I awaited updates and any developments so I could begin preparing any warrants if necessary.

On May 27, 2004, at 2:30 p.m., Dr. George Hudock conducted an autopsy on Carrie Lynn Martin's body.

Carrie was listed as five feet tall and approximately 165 pounds. She had a butterfly tattoo on her right calf. She was dressed in an oversized Nike shirt, worn as a nightshirt. It was soaked in blood and torn from numerous slash and stab wounds.

A pair of blood-soaked panties had been found beneath the shirt, tucked between her arm and torso.

Carrie's body was marked by forty-seven stab and slash wounds across her head, neck, arms, hands, and torso. Both hands showed severe injuries consistent with defensive wounds, with slashes that extended completely through the hand.

The most devastating injuries were to her neck. There were three stab wounds on the left side, each up to seven centimeters deep, extending downward to the fourth cervical vertebra. Her trachea was lacerated on the right side, and her jugular vein had been cut.

There was also a cluster of five stab wounds on the left posterior thoracic wall. A 2.5-centimeter laceration was found on her left ear, and another on her scalp, just above the ear. That wound was so deep, it exposed the cranial bone.

On the left upper anterior thoracic wall, there was a distinct diagonal pattern of bruising—ecchymosis—that resembled a ladder. It measured five centimeters in length and six centimeters in width.

Dr. Hudock determined the cause of death to be multiple stab wounds and the manner of death to be homicide.

Carrie's family members were brought to the state police barracks. Her grandfather, both grandmothers, her mother (Wendy) and father (Tom), and Wendy's husband (Chris) were all there.

I entered the room flanked by the lead troopers and District Attorney Jim McMonagle, a more experienced prosecutor, joined the case with me the day after the murder. Jim was going to lead the case. He was smart and experienced and very matter-of-fact.

I introduced myself and told the family I'd be handling the case alongside Jim. I noticed that Wendy was staring right at me. That is a look I've since come to recognize—the look of a mother whose child has been murdered. It's hollow. It's filled with fear, shock, anger, and sadness all at once. It's also a look that seeks vengeance. If you've ever seen it, you never forget it.

All Wendy wanted me and everyone there to understand was that Carrie would have fought. She said, "Carrie would've fought for her life."

I said, "I understand. I know she did. And this wasn't her fault. She didn't invite this."

The look Wendy had was desperation, but also determination. She was searching for something. What she really wanted to say was, as she later told me: "Just fucking tell me you're going to get this guy."

So I did. I told her, "I'll take care of this." I saw in Wendy a mother who needed my help just like my mother predicted. I was inspired and ready to do so.

CHAPTER 4

JOE AND DAN

ON MAY 27, 2004, DANIEL Kukucka, twenty-six, was living in government housing at the Hilltop Apartments complex on Roosevelt Street in the Pennsylvania borough of Edwardsville. He lived with his girlfriend, Chrisdee, and their children.

They lived in the apartment below Joseph Gacha, also twenty-six, and his fiancée, Heather Sherlinski, along with their children. Kukucka was unemployed. Gacha was working as a cook at the former Kukadoo's Bar in Pittston, Pennsylvania.

Around 3:30 p.m., Gacha asked Kukucka for a ride to work. Kukucka drove him there and returned to the apartment complex. Just before 5 p.m., Heather came downstairs and asked Kukucka if he would pick Joe up from work at 11 p.m.

At around 1:10 a.m., Kukucka woke Chrisdee and told her that Gacha had asked him to go to Larksville. They left around 1:15 a.m. By 6 a.m., Kukucka was back home, asleep on the couch, still wearing the clothes from the night before. Chrisdee assumed that he and Gacha had gone out drinking.

Later that day, around noon, Chrisdee saw the news and learned there had been a murder on Howard Street in Larksville the previous night.

She woke Kukucka and told him. Kukucka immediately responded, "That's where I took Joe (Gacha) last night." Shocked, she asked what he meant. Kukucka explained that they had gone to that address, and when Gacha came back out to the truck, he had blood on his hands.

Soon after, Kukucka's cousin Andy arrived. He told them that his friend Jimmy Burge's girlfriend had been murdered the night before. Kukucka and Andy left the apartment. Kukucka returned around 3:15 p.m.

Around 6 p.m., the phone rang. Chrisdee answered and recognized Gacha's voice. "Put Dan on the phone," he demanded.

The same morning of May 28, just after 6 a.m., Gacha woke Heather and told her to pack up—they were going to the beach. It was an unplanned trip. She hurriedly packed up their children and loaded them into her minivan. Gacha seemed hyper and nervous.

On the way, Gacha said they had to stop at his mother's house in Nanticoke. As they drove, Gacha told Heather there had been a stabbing in Larksville. At first, he said Kukucka had stabbed the girl after they went there to buy weed.

Then he changed the story and said he'd tried to choke the girl and got bitten. Eventually, he told Heather that he and Kukucka had both stabbed her multiple times.

Gacha claimed they'd taken a DVD player and a game console from the scene and sold them at a crack house in Wilkes-Barre. He also said he'd gone back to Kukadoo's and stolen about eight hundred dollars from the register and from the beer cooler. Gacha showed Heather the cash, which she would describe later on as a stack two inches thick.

When they arrived at his mother's house, Gacha showed Heather a bite wound on his left finger, saying, "This is where the bitch bit me."

Inside the house, they were greeted by Gacha's mother, Jacqueline Gacha, his brother Chris, and Jackie's boyfriend, Mike. Gacha immediately pulled Chris into the kitchen, telling him, "I'm in big trouble, brother." He claimed he had killed someone but said it was a man.

Heather simultaneously confided in Jacqueline, saying Gacha had told her he'd killed a woman in Larksville. Gacha came back into the room and, when questioned, exclaimed, "OK, I killed a guy last night."

Heather reminded him that he had said it was a girl. He snapped back, "I'll knock your fucking head off. What did I say to you about things?" Then he pulled off his bandage to show the bite wound.

They stayed a short while longer before leaving. Gacha told his family he, Heather, and the kids had to disappear for a while. Chris and Jackie weren't sure whether to believe him—Gacha often exaggerated. They waited until noon to watch the news and were horrified to see a report confirming the murder. They immediately called the police.

Gacha, Heather, and the children drove to Bristol, Tennessee, arriving at the Econo Lodge around 8:30 p.m. The next morning, they drove to Virginia Beach, arriving around 10 p.m. and staying at another Econo Lodge. They took the kids to the beach the next day.

That evening, they camped in their van near Fort Story in Virginia Beach. The following day, they left around 10 a.m. and drove back to Pennsylvania, arriving after midnight.

Back in Pennsylvania, Gacha tried to rob Kukadoo's again. There was no cash, but he stole checks and attempted to cash one. When it didn't work, Heather said, he literally ate the check. He told her to play dumb and that he was planning to drop the kids off at his mother's before contacting the police. When he arrived, law enforcement was already there.

After Gacha's mother and brother called the police, the investigators quickly learned of his association with Kukucka.

On May 28, 2004, just before 10 p.m., police brought Kukucka in for questioning. He was taken to the Wyoming State Police barracks.

He looked like a zombie—malnourished, tall, hollow-eyed, with dark areas under his eyes and as if he hadn't bathed in weeks. Honestly, he didn't look strong enough to have taken Carrie on. Because what we were learning was that Carrie Martin hadn't just been Luzerne County Fair Queen; she'd been tough. No slouch.

And Kukucka didn't have a scratch on him. That stood out to me. *Whoever did this would have injuries,* I thought.

Luzerne County detective Gary Sworen and trooper Lisa Brogan interviewed Kukucka. After being read his rights, he agreed to speak.

Kukucka told them that when he picked Gacha up from work in his Chevy Blazer, they had talked about wanting to get weed. Kukucka said he knew someone in Larksville who sometimes had it, so they went to Howard Street. He said they weren't planning to pay—they were going to "rip them off."

Kukucka recalled walking into the Music Room. A female voice said, "Come in." It was Jim's girlfriend, Carrie. He asked where Jimmy was, and Carrie told them he was at work. Kukucka asked her for weed. Carrie said she was sick and didn't have any. Kukucka said he got up to leave, thinking Gacha was following behind him.

Instead, Gacha jumped on Carrie and grabbed her by the throat. Kukucka heard her gurgling and yelled at Gacha to stop. He said the next thing he knew, there was blood everywhere—on the floor, the mattress, and Carrie's shirt. Gacha got up, covered in blood, while Carrie lay twitching on her side.

Kukucka ran out and started the Blazer. Gacha came out with a DVD player and an XBOX. They left the area and returned to Hilltop Apartments.

Along the way, Gacha threw out a safe, saying it was empty. Kukucka also said he had dropped a pipe near the scene. Kukucka gave Gacha a white turtleneck sweater to cover up the blood on his arms.

When Kukucka asked if he had killed her, Gacha responded, "She's dead." Kukucka said that Gacha admitted to slitting Carrie's throat three times.

Gacha told Kukucka to say he had only given Gacha and a friend a ride to get weed.

Kukucka told the interviewers that they were back at Hilltop by 12:30 a.m.—just two hours after he had picked Gacha up. He initially left out some details but later admitted to making several stops, including a beer run, an ATM withdrawal, and picking up weed.

Kukucka said they cleaned blood from the Blazer, and that Gacha had ditched something in a dumpster.

On June 2, 2004, at 9:30 a.m., troopers Lisa Brogan and Charles Prula arrived at Gacha's mother's house in Nanticoke. They had been in contact with her for several days, trying to locate Gacha.

As they were speaking with Jackie and Chris, there was a knock at the door.

It was Gacha.

The troopers immediately ordered him to the ground. They handcuffed him on the spot and took him into custody without resistance.

Gacha was transported to the Wyoming State Police barracks. There, he was read his Miranda rights, and he signed a waiver agreeing to speak with Gary and Lisa.

I stood behind the two-way glass when they interviewed him. I saw Gacha for the first time. His hand was badly injured. Carrie had bitten off a chunk of skin. The injury said everything about the brutality of the killing.

Gacha was strong. Tall. Dirty. He looked as if he hadn't showered recently, and he looked tired. Still, he had something in him. A negative aura that reeked of psychosis. He was a dark soul. You just knew this guy was capable of what we'd seen in the Music Room.

He gave a detailed statement: "I, Joseph S. Gacha, was working at Kukadoo's on 5/27/04 and was set to leave work for eleven p.m. Danny Kukucka came to pick me up around ten forty-five, but I didn't get off until eleven. We had two draft beers at the bar before leaving around eleven forty-five or midnight."

Joe said that they then began driving home but started talking about getting weed: "Danny said he needed a blunt but had no money. I told him I'd buy if he found some."

According to Gacha, Kukucka said he knew a place in Larksville. They drove through Pringle and down past the Hilltop Apartments, ending up near the Full Moon Cafe in Larksville. Dan parked on a street in front of a white house.

"As we pulled up," Gacha said, "Danny said, 'If they have a lot of weed, I'm taking it.' I said, 'I got your back.'"

They walked through a garage and into a room where a woman's voice called out, "Who's there?"

Danny answered, "It's me, Dan."

She told them to turn on the light. Gacha found the switch behind the door. The woman—Carrie Martin—was lying on a mattress on the floor.

"Danny sat down and asked, 'Where's the weed?'" Gacha told the interviewers. "She said, 'I don't got none.' Gacha asked for the lockbox, saw it, and reached for it. She grabbed his arm."

Gacha said he stepped forward, grabbing her face and arm to pull her back. That's when she bit him on the finger.

"I let go," he said, "and Danny pulled a knife from his pocket. He stabbed her twice, cutting her face and neck."

Gacha admitted to throwing Carrie onto the mattress to get her away from Kukucka but said that Kukucka followed her and continued stabbing.

"She said, 'Please don't. I'm pregnant.'"

Gacha claimed he grabbed the lockbox and carried it outside to Kukucka's truck, then came back inside.

Carrie was now lying face down on the floor.

"Dan said she was still moving, and started stomping on her head," Gacha said.

Gacha believed she was dead at that point. But he took the knife from Kukucka and stabbed her three more times in the lower back.

"To make sure she wasn't suffering," he said.

He handed the knife back to Kukucka, who then picked up a blue guitar. Gacha grabbed an XBOX and a DVD player. They both ran out.

Gacha said that on the way back, Kukucka told him he would get rid of the evidence—the clothes, electronics, and knife.

Gacha changed out of his bloody clothes at home, leaving his shorts at the bottom of some steps. He said at the time of the crime that he was wearing brown cargo shorts and a gray Tasmanian Devil T-shirt. Gacha said Kukucka was wearing a white T-shirt, baggy blue jeans, and Skechers.

Gacha ended his statement by claiming they tried to get weed from another dealer afterward, but that nothing had come of it. The interview ended.

When officers led Gacha out of the interview room, our eyes locked. It was the first time I'd ever looked a killer in the eyes. The hair on the back of my neck stood up. I had seen what he'd done. I didn't feel tough; I felt like I was reacting appropriately to the horror of what I'd seen.

It was on. Gacha and Kukucka were now my focus.

But Gacha. He was the one who stood out to me. My instincts told me Gacha was the principal in this killing and I was going to hold him responsible.

Later, in addition to the evidence that grass cutter Thomas Kurisky had found—Carrie's purse, the clothing, and the IRS check—investigators recovered the seat covers from the Blazer. They found one in a dumpster outside the Hilltop Apartments complex and the other inside Kukucka and Chrisdee's apartment.

The seat cover from the dumpster was stained with blood.

This evidence, combined with Gacha's and Kukucka's partial admissions, physical evidence, and witness statements, helped investigators piece together the full picture of what had happened inside the Music Room on the night Carrie Martin was murdered and who was responsible.

CHAPTER 5

MORE DEATH

ON JUNE 14, 2004, JIMMY Burge sat quietly on his grandmother's back porch.

For weeks after Carrie's murder, he hadn't been able to bring himself to step back into the Music Room. He just stared at it—day after day—trying to make sense of the emptiness left behind.

The room had once been filled with sound, life, and plans. Now, it was a shell. He had been staying on the porch, looking from a distance, haunted.

His father, Jim Sr., joined him outside. He put a hand on Jimmy's shoulder, offering quiet comfort.

"You don't have to go back in there," he told his son.

Jimmy nodded. Jim Sr. asked him to sign a birthday card for his grandmother. They then had dinner together—bread and gravy—and afterward, Jimmy stepped onto the front porch and began playing his guitar.

Around 7 p.m., Jimmy heard something from inside the house. A thud. He rushed in.

His father had collapsed. A massive heart attack. Jim Burge Sr. was dead; he was only fifty-three.

Less than six weeks later, on July 22, 2004, Kukucka was found slumped over, a sheet wrapped tightly around his neck and secured to a bookshelf. He had leaned forward and hanged himself. He had killed himself.

Kukucka had left behind a suicide note. In it, he apologized to the corrections officers who would find him. He asked that all of his belongings—sealed in a manila envelope—be sent to Chrisdee. He said he couldn't do it anymore. Couldn't be in that place, in that state, under that weight.

He claimed his innocence. Said he never touched Carrie. That he had no idea that Gacha had been planning to rob her. The only crime he admitted to was giving a maniac a ride to buy weed from, as he wrote, "a harmless, great person who didn't deserve to die."

He begged the system not to fail in holding Gacha accountable.

Now, he said, two innocent people were dead because of Gacha. He wrote that he couldn't keep going—couldn't live like this, losing his family, losing his life, and failing those who needed him.

He said that he wished he had been stronger. But he wasn't.

He said he would never forgive himself.

CHAPTER 6

THE PROSECUTION BEGINS

ON AUGUST 12, 2004, GACHA'S preliminary hearing was held before the Honorable John Hasay. This was my first homicide proceeding in court. I was seated at the table with Assistant District Attorney Jim McMonagle, Gary Sworen, and Lisa Brogan. We presented Lisa Brogan; Deputy Coroner Bill Lisman; Gacha's fiancé, Heather Sherlinski; and some additional witnesses. Jim let me handle most of the witnesses. All criminal charges against Gacha were bound over to the Luzerne County Court of Common Pleas.

Conflict counsel Mark Bufalino and Paul Galante represented Gacha during the preliminary hearing.

In the weeks following the preliminary hearing, District Attorney Lupas then assigned Jim McMonagle to the prosecution of Hugo Selenski, a case you will hear more about later. Assistant District Attorney Bill Finnegan replaced him on the Gacha prosecution team.

Bill Finnegan had a great reputation and had prosecuted several homicides in the office. I was happy to be working with him and knew the case was in good hands.

On February 10, 2005, Heather Sherlinski met with our team. She was trying to rebuild her life. She told us that, at one point, she asked Gacha who had actually done it. He leaned in close to her and whispered, "I did."

She said he told her he'd covered Carrie's mouth and "slit her throat." When she asked him why, and how he could do something so brutal, he just shrugged and said, "I don't know. I just went blank."

Heather told investigators that Gacha hadn't even known Carrie's name at the time, and that he blamed Kukucka, claiming that Kukucka had told him it would be an easy place to get drugs and money. Gacha had told Heather that Kukucka had stabbed Carrie, too.

While they were on the run, Gacha had told Heather, "She was a hard bitch to kill."

Heather also disclosed that Gacha had beaten her in the past. He was volatile when he drank or smoked weed. She told us that she was trying to straighten her life out and she was adapting to life without the volatile Gacha.

CHAPTER 7

BUILDING THE CASE IN BLOOD

AS WE BEGAN TO BUILD the case against Gacha and prepare for trial, it became clear that we needed to tell a compelling story—one that proved he wasn't just an accomplice. He was the principal. The one who had done the killing.

Bill Finnigan successfully prosecuted a homicide case in 2002, working with a forensic consultant named Paul Kish. When Bill reviewed the evidence in Carrie's case, he believed that Kish could help us again. He told me to handle it and get everything to Kish as soon as possible. To this day, Bill keeps a to-do list. When you are assigned an item on Bill's to-do list and he crosses it off his list, you had better get it done. I was entrusted with the blood spatter presentation.

I dug in.

I learned that Paul Kish was from Bradford, New York. He held a degree in criminal justice and had extensive experience in bloodstain pattern analysis and crime scene reconstruction. He'd consulted on over a thousand homicide cases across nearly all fifty states and thirteen countries.

Kish was the real deal.

I asked him to review the blood evidence from the Music Room—on the scene, on Gacha's clothing, and especially the bloodstains left on the crossmember, a wooden board that was affixed to the exterior of the door. We believed his analysis could confirm that Gacha wasn't a bystander, that he was the man who had stabbed Carrie Martin to death.

I mailed him a binder of lab reports, police documents, and photos.

In November 2004, Kish traveled to Northeastern Pennsylvania to meet with our team. I was immediately impressed. He had a complete grasp of the facts and knew exactly what we needed.

We brought him to the Music Room so he could get a sense of the layout. Afterward, we returned to the state police barracks, where Kish set up a mobile lab with tarps and special lighting. He got to work like a mad scientist.

He laid out the clothing that Gacha, Kukucka, and Carrie had been wearing. Gacha's short-sleeve denim shirt. A pair of cargo shorts. A white T-shirt. The white sweater that Kukucka claimed he'd given to Gacha. Kukucka's pin-striped shirt and jeans. And Carrie's blood-soaked Nike T-shirt, now dried and hardened from saturation.

Regarding the crime scene, Kish described Carrie's body as lying face down between a mattress on the floor and a nearby sofa. There was no bed frame—just the mattress on the floor. She had been clad in a T-shirt saturated with blood, and the shirt had visible tears across the back.

Kish noted that Carrie had suffered numerous stab and slash wounds, including extensive defensive wounds on both hands. He was aware of the horrific injuries to her neck as well: lacerations to the trachea, jugular veins, and carotid artery.

He described the bottom bedsheet near her body as being heavily soaked in blood. There was also a transfer pattern on the lower sheet, likely from a shoe sole. Blood was evident on the pillows as well as on a comforter at the head of the bed, all bearing heavy staining.

A pillowcase lying on top of Carrie's lower body had the same pattern as the bedsheet and was also soaked in blood. Nearby blankets and other linen items on the sofa adjacent to Carrie's body were similarly stained.

Spatter was present on the wall behind her, extending from the sofa on her left side across to a section above the bed on her right. The blood patterns and directionality confirmed that Carrie had been cut and bled in that immediate area, and only there.

Then came the crossmember on the Music Room door.

Kish concluded that the bloodstains were consistent with a transfer mechanism. Testing revealed that the DNA matched Gacha's. It showed that he had been bleeding, touched the door, and left the blood behind as he exited.

Gacha's denim shirt told its own story.

Transfer stains covered the front, including both the inside and outside of the button placket. Blood spatter was prominent across the upper chest and the right sleeve. Spatter was found even under the pocket flap, meaning that there had been movement and contact at the moment the blood landed.

A sample collected from the shirt tested positive for human blood. The DNA matched Carrie's.

To Kish, the evidence was undeniable. Gacha hadn't just been in the room; he'd been in contact with Carrie as she bled. He'd been close enough during the stabbing to be covered in her blood.

Kish turned to Gacha's cargo shorts. They bore transfer stains on the front and inside the right pocket. Spatter marked the lower-left leg. A sample taken from the upper-right front tested positive for human blood. The DNA matched Gacha's.

Gacha's white T-shirt had transfer stains on the front as well as other areas on the outside, and on the inside, too. DNA analysis confirmed it was Carrie's blood.

The white sweater had heavy transfer staining inside both sleeves, particularly at the cuffs. There was no spatter, just transfer stains. This aligned with Kukucka's statement that Gacha had worn it after the killing. Blood from Gacha's arms had rubbed off onto the fabric.

The pin-striped shirt that Kukucka had worn that night had no visible blood, not a drop. His jeans, however, did have transfer stains around the lower legs. They were consistent with stomping or kicking.

Then came the ladder pattern on Carrie's neck, a strange, confounding bruise. It caught the eye of Detective Gary Sworen as he studied crime scene photographs. Then he zoomed in on Gacha's cargo shorts and saw the cause.

The zippers.

The teeth on the cargo shorts' zippered pockets aligned with the ladder bruise on Carrie's neck. The zippers were swabbed and tested. Carrie's DNA was there.

That bruise wasn't random. It was the mark left when Gacha's body came into forceful contact with her neck—the imprint left behind by a zipper pressing into her skin as he stabbed her. It was the final link in a chain of forensic evidence that painted the full picture.

Gacha hadn't been a passive observer. He hadn't just walked into a scene. He'd created it. He had stabbed Carrie, pressed down on her, and left part of his clothing behind as a fingerprint on her body.

There was no more room for doubt, and the jury would have to understand this deeply.

CHAPTER 8

THE TRIAL

ON SEPTEMBER 8, 2006, AFTER many starts and stops, we finally prosecuted Gacha. During those years leading up to the trial, I would meet with Wendy and her family. Delays are tough as cases move forward. Wendy would always look to me to assure her that it was going to be OK and that the delay wouldn't hurt us. I would always take time to talk with her one-on-one to make sure she knew we weren't forgetting about Carrie and her case was a top priority. I spent the two years preparing and trying other cases. Gacha remained in his jail cell awaiting trial.

Nicole and I were expecting our first child. She was due just four weeks after the trial began. We knew we were having a boy and decided his name was Dominick. The morning of the first day, Nicole gave me an envelope and a kiss on the cheek. She said, "Open it before you start the trial."

I opened it and there was a card inside. The front of the card had the name Dominick Ferentino. It looked like professional stationery. I smiled and opened it. The note inside said, "Good luck, Daddy. You're going to do great! I love you and I will see you soon. Love, Dominick." My eyes welled up. I was ready.

The case was a death penalty case. Gacha was accused of killing Carrie during a robbery, which qualified the case as a capital prosecution.

Bill Finnegan gave me the opportunity to handle major witnesses. He did the opening and closing arguments. I had the opportunity to question people, including Paul Kish, Wendy, and Heather. These were huge witnesses. It made me feel like a lead prosecutor at such an early point in my career, trying a death penalty case.

And I loved it. I loved every bit of it—the adrenaline, the fear, the stakes. I would meticulously plan my suits and ties. I would make sure my posture was straight and my shoulders were back. I would shine my shoes every night, which was one of the few memories I had of my father. I always looked at the suits and my style as a way to show the jury I was confident and prepared. The anxiety leading up to the trial washed away as the trial began. Bill and our team prepared for many months and were more than ready for our case.

Throughout the trial, I would meet with Wendy and her family. I would reassure them that the case was going according to plan and that we were in good shape.

Judge Joseph Augello presided over the trial. Judge Augello was always calm and professional. He is a good judge and a gentleman.

One thing that has stuck with me to this day is the talks with Heather. She was a broken woman and mother. She had her own problems—substance issues, emotional instability.

But I learned something from prepping her. My working with her made her a better witness. Getting her comfortable helped. And as time went on, she moved further away from Gacha—emotionally, psychologically.

And I'll never forget when we learned that Gacha had said about Carrie, "She was a hard bitch to kill." Those words haunted me and continue to haunt me today.

We fought to get that line into evidence. Over the defense's objections, I pushed to make sure the jury heard that more than once. When I sat down next to Bill after getting the statement in repeatedly, he said, "Good job, they got it."

Carrie had bitten Gacha. He'd been caked in her blood. His DNA was on the crossmember board when he left. He'd fled the scene.

And she'd fought like hell.

That told me everything I needed to know about Carrie Martin. She'd fought with everything she had. And that mattered in the courtroom.

During the trial, there was an exchange between direct examination of Paul Kish and cross-examination. There was a dispute over a conclusion of Kish's over a point that he couldn't definitively conclude Gacha was the killer, only that he was in close proximity to Carrie when she was stabbed. On redirect, I made a stabbing motion with my hand, saying, "Within this far?" clearly demonstrating Gacha was close enough to kill and had stabbed Carrie. It made a clear point over the defense's questions. Kish said yes. I said, "No further questions."

Bill Finnegan was impressed and laughing, whispered, "You just became a trial lawyer. Nice job."

Jimmy Burge also testified. He told the jury about Carrie's life together. He laid out their final day and listed the items that were stolen from the Music Room. He has gone on in his life and is a celebrated local musician known as "Jimmy Stranger." He wrote a song about that time and the impact of losing Carrie, Jimmy Sr., and his grandmother, called "Sixteen Ounces." I am happy to note he stays in touch with Wendy.

Attorneys Mark Bufalino and John Pike represented Gacha throughout the trial. Both are very capable and professional. As predicted, they tried to paint Kukucka as the principal. It didn't work.

The jury convicted Gacha of first-degree criminal homicide, robbery, theft by unlawful taking, and criminal conspiracy.

Justice had arrived. Late, but certain.

When the jury convicted Gacha, we moved into the penalty phase. We were going to ask the jury to impose the death penalty.

We put on aggravators—how brutal the murder was, how young Carrie had been, how it had occurred during a robbery. Then the defense got a chance to tell Gacha's life story, including mitigators: mental health, abuse, brain injuries, that kind of thing.

They brought in a psychiatrist. Talked about some head trauma Gacha had. Discussed educational records. And then they brought in his second-grade teacher, who said that one Halloween, Gacha hadn't had a Halloween costume, so the staff bought him a little tiger costume.

I thought, "Maybe this tugs on the jury's heartstrings."

Maybe it did. Because they didn't impose the death penalty.

Joseph Gacha's life was spared, but under Pennsylvania law, he was automatically sentenced to life imprisonment without the possibility of parole. On top of that, he was sentenced to ten to twenty years, consecutive, for the robbery, and another ten to twenty years, consecutive, for the criminal conspiracy. The theft charge was merged with the others.

I was OK with all of that.

I didn't need a death sentence. I wanted a conviction. I needed him gone forever.

I occasionally shared a passing glance with Gacha during the trial, but I wasn't focused on him as a person—I was focused on Wendy and finding justice for her.

Gacha showed no remorse, only anger and frustration. He never apologized after his conviction. He continued to blame Kukucka.

After the trial, we convened in the basement of the courthouse. Our team hugged one another in celebration. Wendy and her family joined us. I gave Wendy a hug and talked with the rest of her family. I was exhausted but proud of our team. I knew we couldn't bring Carrie back, but I hoped putting Gacha away forever would give Wendy some peace.

CHAPTER 9

A MOM AND A KILLER, FACE-TO-FACE

FOLLOWING THE CASE, WENDY WOULD call my private office on occasion to say hello or to check in. I enjoyed staying in touch and knowing she was doing OK. She was following my career and would always compliment me on a case from the newspaper. I was honored to have her follow my career.

Wendy became an advocate for victims. I was happy that she was working on helping other victims. She had joined a group of other parents whose children were murdered. They advocated for victims and would counsel one another. One day, she called and said she was going to arrange a meeting with Gacha. I asked, "Why? What do you think you will find there or in him?"

She said, "I just feel like I have some things to say to him."

I didn't understand, but I said, "If you believe that's something you want and that can help, then go for it."

Wendy wanted answers and a chance to say what she'd never had the chance to say during the trial. It took nine months of coordination. Gacha had to agree. Counselors and a psychiatrist would be present. Wendy arranged a face-to-face meeting with Gacha on December 10, 2009, at the State Correctional

Institution (SCI) Greensburg, a medium-security, all-male correctional institution in Pennsylvania.

Wendy came to see me and told me all about the visit. On that December day, Wendy traveled with Tammy Burke from the Victims Resources Center in Wilkes-Barre to the prison.

When they arrived, a corrections officer led her to a small room. The officer asked Wendy where she'd like to sit.

"I'll sit near the wall," she said. "Not by the door."

Wendy didn't want Gacha to think she needed an easy escape route. She didn't want him to think she was afraid.

The meeting lasted four hours.

Gacha was uncuffed. They sat face-to-face, not separated by glass. At first, Wendy froze. She couldn't feel herself breathe. She couldn't speak. But after a few minutes of silence, she said, she felt the hand of God on her shoulder, and she began to relax.

She asked Gacha questions—about his family, about prison life.

He told her he was doing well. He had converted to Buddhism. He was coaching basketball inside the prison.

He didn't volunteer much information, but he answered whatever she asked. He told her he was tattooing other inmates. The way they made ink, he said, was by melting plastic checkers. They used the hardened, melted plastic as ink.

Then Wendy cut through the small talk. She asked him directly about the murder. He continued to blame Kukucka.

When she pressed him, asking how Carrie bit him, he didn't respond.

At one point, Wendy told him, "My other daughter is the same age as your son. What if they meet? What if he has to tell her, 'My father killed your sister'?"

Gacha didn't respond. Instead, he started talking about how everyone in his life had betrayed him. He claimed that even his mother and brother had turned on him. "They never cared for me," he said.

Wendy had brought pictures of Carrie with her. She laid them out on the table so he could see them.

He closely scanned each one, except one. He placed his hand over the image of Carrie's tombstone and wouldn't look at it.

Toward the end of the meeting, Gacha finally asked her, "Why did you want to do this?"

Wendy responded with calm precision. "When you said she was a hard bitch to kill, you were talking about my daughter," she said. "I'm no different. Livestock led by a butcher to the slaughter was given more mercy than what you gave her."

Coffee was served near the end of the meeting. Wendy watched as Gacha's hands trembled. He kept carelessly dumping sugar into the cup.

She felt as though her words had gotten through.

He had shaken her hand at the start of the meeting. But now, seeing him shake, she stood up and walked away.

There was no yelling. No dramatics. Just words—and then silence.

Afterward, the psychiatrist in attendance pulled Wendy aside and said, "That went as well as one of these meetings ever could."

What kind of mother sits face-to-face with the man who butchered her daughter?

A strong one. A broken one. A mother still holding every shattered piece of herself together by sheer will.

Wendy didn't go to SCI Greensburg for forgiveness. She went for control—for clarity. For the chance to say what the courtroom hadn't given her space to say. Not with rage, but with calm, deliberate words that cut deeper than any outburst ever could.

I believe she went there as a representative for every mother who never gets a resolution. For every family that sits across the dinner table from an empty chair. For every parent who turns a bedroom into a shrine. For every woman who lies awake at night with the image of her child's last moments playing on a loop in her mind.

Wendy faced Joseph Gacha not as a victim, but as a force.

He trembled. She did not.

In a room built for confrontation, she found something else: resolve. Not healing, not peace. But power. The kind that can come only from surviving the unimaginable and speaking truth to the man who had tried to erase her daughter's existence.

Carrie's murder didn't silence Wendy. It sharpened her.

Some murders end lives. Others forge warriors.

• • •

December 30, 2019—ten years after Wendy's visit. Joseph Gacha, forty-two years old, was spending the rest of his natural life in prison. After SCI Greensburg closed in 2013, he was moved to SCI Fayette, Pennsylvania. That December evening, he began acting violently and erratically.

Gacha attacked his cellmate. His behavior escalated—he displayed a level of strength and rage that forced prison security to restrain him. He was strapped into a restraint chair, then transported to the infirmary.

Even there, Gacha continued to fight. Ambulance personnel were called. They arrived at the prison and tried to assist, but Gacha never regained control. Despite efforts to subdue him, he died at 9:39 p.m., following the altercations.

Prison officials speculated that Gacha may have ingested K2, a synthetic form of marijuana, smuggled into the prison. To date, the coroner's office has not publicly released a conclusive cause of death.

Lisa Brogan called me to tell me that Gacha was dead. I felt nothing initially.

The following morning, I was on a treadmill at the gym. I looked up, and there was a report on the television regarding Gacha's death. My heart raced when I saw his image, I have to admit.

And I thought, *I handled this case from the moment of the killing to the literal graves of the killers.*

And my only hope, in that moment, was that his death had brought Wendy peace.

I didn't feel vindicated. I didn't celebrate.

I just hoped it helped Wendy.

CHAPTER 10

HORROR AT WORK AND HAPPINESS AT HOME

THE GACHA CASE BEGAN IN May 2004 and went to trial in September 2006. I was engaged and married in May 2005 to my wife, Nicole. She is beautiful and intelligent and has proven to be an amazing wife and mother.

Fortunately, the trial didn't overlap with the wedding, but Wendy was excited that I was getting married. There was a friendship there, a kinship. And some prosecutors would tell you that's a mistake.

Guess what? F those prosecutors. If I don't care, I can't care. If I don't care, I won't care.

I chose to care for this family, especially Wendy. I saw my own mother in her. My grandmothers. Wendy became part of my motivation. She was the model for the mothers and victims who followed over the next twenty years.

In court, she would lean on me, physically lean into me, and I loved that. She had victim resource people with her, but I'd push past them and go straight to her. I don't deal with intermediaries. I deal with the people who need help.

And Wendy has told me that it meant everything to her. Every time I saw her, she looked as if she'd just been crying for hours.

As if she were at her wits' end. But once in a while, I'd make her smile and laugh. And that mattered.

Keeping her informed—whether the news was good, bad, or indifferent—and telling her it was going to be OK, that we were going to get this guy, was part of the job.

Gacha went to trial in September 2006, as noted earlier. My son Dominick was born in October 2006, so Nicole was in the last stage of pregnancy during the trial. I kept my phone with me in case she went into labor.

I remember that when Dominick was born, I held him in the hospital and suddenly understood what Wendy had gone through. How death teaches you about new life.

And I thought, *You have to be careful when you take on evil like murder*. Because now, holding this baby, I realized that I had an Achilles heel. Evil people could come after him. I was vulnerable now.

Many friends and even detectives showed up at the hospital. One of them, Detective Gary Capitano, came in and saw me holding Dominick. He said, "I hope this doesn't make you soft now."

I told him, "No, Gary. This is going to make me harder. Don't worry." And he jokingly said, "By the way, that baby looks Irish." We both laughed.

As I held Dominick, Gacha continually returned to mind. I think it had to do with the fact that we were fighting to take his life. He was facing the death penalty.

And there I was, holding a newborn in my arms, thinking about death. The mental shift from courtroom battle to birthing room was jarring. But it was real.

During that time, I was happy to share my wedding and becoming a father with Wendy's family. They weren't literally there for those events, but they were part of that moment in my life. It mattered. I was growing—becoming a husband, a father—

and simultaneously preparing to prosecute this monster. Wendy and her family were woven into that evolution.

After Jim McMonagle left the case, they assigned Bill Finnegan early on, around June 2003. Bill was a part-time assistant district attorney, about fifteen years older than me. He'd just done a big case at the office, and he had a reputation.

Bill always looked busy. His life was a to-do list. He had five kids and was an Eagle Scout, extremely organized, and humble—the opposite of who I thought I was becoming at the time. Bill is an amazing father and husband.

He worked hard and ran marathons. I lifted weights at the time, but I started running with Bill, and we'd talk during those runs about preparing the Gacha case. That's how I got into running, which I have been doing daily since.

Bill became a mentor to me. He was a tough coach. When it was time for an "attaboy," he'd give you five more things to do.

So, getting a compliment from him? That meant something. I was proud of that.

Today, Bill Finnegan is my law partner. He brought me into his law firm after the Gacha case. I think at first, he was trying to figure out if I was legit or just a big talker.

But he taught me how to prepare a murder case. He drilled into me that the evidence has to match the elements of the crime like a puzzle. That your witnesses must know what's coming. That you better not get caught up in a flash before building the foundation. He was disciplined.

I still use his methods. We were opposites, but we had the same mission. We weren't afraid to roll up our sleeves. And we made a damn good team.

Most of Bill's children have since served as babysitters for my two children at one time or another.

Bill and I have built a law firm that has and continues to serve Northeastern Pennsylvania for over twenty years. That partnership was born from the Carrie Martin case.

From that fight. That's a legacy.

And as for Wendy? We still talk. She was and still is important to me.

That meeting with Gacha, for Wendy, was about reclaiming something that was stolen. And I realized that it's important for mothers of victims to reclaim power even if their hearts are broken. Even if they're never whole again, they need to find a way to say, "You don't control me. You didn't destroy me. I will survive."

And in this case, Gacha didn't survive. Wendy did.

During the investigation, we'd monitored Gacha's phone calls from jail. He'd talked about trying to escape during transport. Said he was going to punch me in the face. Said I was corrupt. That he hated me. That he'd punch Gary Sworen, too. Said Lisa Brogan was a bitch.

I loved hearing that, because it meant we were getting to him. He was frustrated. He was angry. And he knew, deep down, we were going to take him down.

And we did.

So let's go back for a moment, to the beginning, to what really motivated me.

The more I learned about Carrie Martin, the more I knew she truly was an innocent victim. She'd worked with disabled children. There's a photo of her on a horse, holding a little girl with disabled arms. I think about that picture a lot. That photo symbolizes everything those two monsters, Gacha and Kukucka, took from the world.

Carrie was special. She'd been raised by Wendy, who worked hard to give Carrie a good life. Carrie had been a leader in school, a role model. She'd been the Luzerne County Fair Queen—literally a queen.

People often say murder victims had a smile that lit up a room. With Carrie, that wasn't just something people said—it was documented. She had a proven record of kindness, of being someone who made a difference.

And that's the tragedy. This wasn't just a murder. This was a capital murder. This was the execution of someone who had made the world better.

And that's why I pushed so hard.

One thing I didn't expect was how, as a prosecutor, I had to become an expert in blood spatter, transfer patterns, and trauma science. Especially working with someone like Paul Kish.

I had to reanimate the scene in my mind. Relive it. Understand it. And then walk into a courtroom and make a jury understand it.

That meant reliving the horror regularly.

I couldn't stop thinking about how hard Carrie had fought. She'd bitten Gacha's hand. She'd clawed, bled. I thought about the ladder mark on her neck, from where her head had been pressed against his side pocket as he stabbed her. The footprints on her body. They'd stomped on her. Stepped on her. On a human being. Someone they didn't even know, whose name they didn't even know.

Gacha called her a bitch. Said she was a "hard bitch to kill." Even after the murder, they were still dehumanizing her.

That alone is why Gacha should have been locked away forever. And honestly? Deserved death.

The biggest takeaway for me, however, is Wendy.

Wendy's confronting Gacha years later was about power. Her goal was to show him, *You didn't break me*. She wanted him to know she was as tough as Carrie.

Wendy was the first mom I ever fought for. You need something to drive you in cases like these—something bigger than yourself—and she was my driving force.

And I trained for this case like it was a war. I lost weight. I ran up to eight miles a day. I'd rarely run even a mile before this case. But I ran to prepare. To think. To stay sharp. To stay ready.

This case set the standard. The model for how I'd handle every prosecution after it.

And Wendy—she was the first. The one who taught me why we fight.

LESSONS IN MOTIVATION FROM THE FAIR QUEEN MURDER

What drives a person to kill a woman like Carrie Martin—an innocent, beloved daughter who did nothing more than trust the wrong person?

That question haunted me throughout this case. And the answer didn't come easily.

I learned that real motivation to go after killers isn't born in the big moments. It's forged in silence. It's built when you're alone at your desk at 11 p.m., flipping through old reports, trying to find the one thing no one else saw, or running and listening to conversations over and over. It's choosing to walk toward the pain, not away from it.

What do you do when you're tasked with delivering justice for someone who can't speak for themselves? When the memory of a daughter, a niece, a friend, rests in your hands?

You commit. You go all in. And when people doubt you—when they doubt the case, the evidence, the victim—you fight harder.

PRACTICAL STEPS: STAYING THE COURSE WHEN YOU'RE ON A MISSION

Let me break this down not from a legal standpoint, but from the trenches of purpose-driven work.

The kind where the stakes are high, the payoff is uncertain, and the burden is heavy.

Own the Mission

You don't get to justice, or to any goal that matters, by going halfway. If you're not all in, get out. Passion without ownership is just noise.

Out-Prepare Everyone

I lived inside this case. I fell asleep reading transcripts, listened to interviews on my runs, and could recite details in my sleep. Success favors those who make the mission a daily ritual. This became the template for what was to come in my career.

Isolate the Signal in the Noise

The world is full of distractions. Headlines, critics, internal office politics—they'll try to pull you off course. Tune them out. Protect the signal—your mission.

Trust Isn't Given; It's Built

I built trust with the victim's family one conversation at a time. You build your reputation the same way—in quiet moments when no one's watching.

Take the Hits, Then Stand Back Up

The justice system isn't designed to make things easy. Neither is life. But both respect those who get back up. Every setback in this case made the conviction more meaningful.

Rehearse the Win

Before I stepped into the courtroom, I had already tried the case in my head a hundred times. Visualize success—not in vague, motivational-poster terms but in tactical, specific details.

Stay Human

It's easy to become cold, especially in dark work. But I went home to my wife and my kids, and let them see the weight I carried. Purpose doesn't require perfection; it requires presence.

Your Story Is the Legacy

I was honored to help tell Carrie's story. You're always telling a story. Make sure it's one you'd be proud to reread.

There Is No "After" Without the Now

Everyone wants the payoff, but no one wants the years of groundwork. My "victory" moment in this case came after years of grinding in obscurity. You don't skip that part.

PRACTICAL STEPS TOWARD RELENTLESS DRIVE

No case ever teaches you everything. But some cases teach you enough to change the way you move through the world.

Carrie's case did that for me. It sharpened my instincts, tested my limits, and deepened my understanding of what it really means to fight for justice, for truth, for someone who can't speak anymore.

This is the biggest lesson I took with me, and the principle I still carry today: *Make it personal—but stay professional.* Carrie reminded me of my own family. That connection made it personal. But I couldn't let that cloud my judgment. My job was to take the emotion and funnel it into focus. If you don't know how to walk that line, the system will eat you alive.

Book 2

THE MOTHER WHO FORGAVE THE MURDERER

Commonwealth v. Donnell Buckner

"Forgiveness is the fragrance the violet sheds on the heel that has crushed it."

—Mark Twain

CHAPTER 1

A FAMILY ON EDGE

THE DONNELL BUCKNER CASE HAS stayed with me because of its stark truths about control, resilience, and the profound power of forgiveness.

March 2009, Wilkes-Barre, Pennsylvania. The Buckners—Donnell, age thirty-five, and his wife, Kewaii Rogers Buckner, thirty-one, were living in a volatile situation that was teetering on the edge of catastrophe.

The Buckners had moved to Wilkes-Barre after being uprooted by a storm in Mississippi. They had three children: two daughters, twelve and eleven, and a nine-year-old son.

Donnell was a man consumed by his own insecurities, disguising his failures with a veneer of control and violence. He stood six feet two inches tall and weighed well north of three hundred pounds.

Kewaii, on the other hand, stood five feet eight inches tall. She was a beautiful Black woman of quiet strength who smiled widely and with her eyes.

She balanced work, school, and motherhood with grace despite living under the weight of her husband's relentless abuse. She was a nursing student, worked as a respiratory therapist, and was the sole pillar holding her family together, as the rest of her immediate family remained in Mississippi.

Kewaii finally reached a breaking point and sought a Protection From Abuse (PFA) order, taking a step that many women in her position only dream of. She turned her private nightmare into a public declaration of her worth.

She went to the Luzerne County Courthouse and wrote down the horrors she'd endured, putting words to years of suffering. This was an act of courage, bravery, and desperation.

Kewaii wrote the following in her PFA petition (edited for clarity):

> Mr. Donnell Buckner threatened my life by saying that I should leave all my money in the bank for the kids because I won't need it. I said to him that if you're going to shoot me then just shoot me because I am tired of your threats and I can't take it anymore.
>
> He said yeah yeah you will see. Also on March 25, 2009. Mr. Buckner asked me if I would like to play a game of Russian roulette and I replied to him that no I do not. I was sitting in my living room next to the door in the event he tried to pull out his gun on me.
>
> He then said close the door I stated no I will not close the door but he insisted so. I was afraid I went back on my porch afterwards he locked me outside of the house when my oldest daughter came home from school, which was around 250. He unlocked the door. Mr. Buckner is very adamant about keeping me in Pennsylvania. He consistently tells me that he will hurt me if I leave him.

He takes all the keys to the vehicles that are in my name so I can't get away. He states if I leave, he will find me and if he doesn't find me, he will kill my parents. On June 28, 2008 Mr. Buckner pushed me down a flight of steps which I had to go to the emergency room. After this, I was assigned a Children And Youth worker because of the incident and the kids talking about the abuse I had been receiving. On October 6, 2008, Mr. Buckner pulled a gun on me and threaten to kill me there were two more times that he pulled a gun on me, but I am unsure of the dates in January. Mr. Buckner pulled the gun on me on the third level of our home and shot into the couch and the bullet is lodged in the floor, he took me into the bedroom where I was begging for my life.

He stated that he knows that someone heard the shot and if the police come, he would blow my head off and then kill himself by the time they come in he said it would be all over and they couldn't protect me. I am afraid to sleep at night because he is so very unstable and I don't know what he will do.

It is not easy to write these things down for others to read.

For abusers like Donnell, Kewaii's act of defiance—her assertion of control—was the ultimate betrayal. And as I've seen time and again in these cases, this moment of triumph can also be the most dangerous moment.

The PFA was issued by a family court judge—a temporary reprieve that was both empowering and terrifying. Kewaii's friends later shared that she knew what was coming. She told them, "He's going to kill me." Can you imagine living with that kind of certainty? And yet, she went on.

CHAPTER 2

THE NIGHT EVERYTHING CHANGED

KEWAII TOOK HER KIDS TO church on Sunday, March 29, 2009. It wasn't their usual routine, but maybe she needed a touch of grace, a moment to anchor herself. When they got home, she returned to the ordinary rhythms of Sunday family life—laundry, chores, a family movie night with *Forrest Gump* playing on the TV.

But that ordinariness was about to shatter.

Donnell kept calling the house. He called more than forty times that Sunday, demanding that Kewaii drop the PFA.

Donnell, known by the nickname "Smokey," came through the back door of their home around 9 p.m. Kewaii, always the protector, sent her children upstairs. What unfolded next was a nightmare that would forever change those children's lives.

Donnell begged her to drop the PFA. Kewaii refused and begged him to leave. When words failed, he pulled out a gun. The children, slowly creeping downstairs, eavesdropped and eventually watched as the argument escalated. They bore witness to his rage.

"Is this what you want?" he screamed as he fired the first shot.

Kewaii, even in her last moments, pleaded with him. "Smokey, stop. Smokey, stop." But he didn't stop. The first shot shattered her arm as she tried to shield herself. The next tore through her head.

Their daughter, just twelve years old, would later recount in painful detail how her mother's pleas echoed through the house after the first loud boom—then a second—and then silence fell.

Kewaii's body was sprawled across the couch and floor, surrounded by the typical items of a Sunday night at home. A laundry basket lay nearby. The TV was still on. But nothing else was typical. The teeth that once shone when she smiled had been blown from her mouth and were scattered on the couch. Pieces of her flesh clung to the dryer in an adjacent room.

The children, still trembling, called 911.

"My father just killed my mother," the oldest said with a steadiness that belied her years.

Donnell fled in the family minivan.

Wilkes-Barre police officer Joe Ziegler, the first on the scene, walked up the driveway along the side of the house and spotted a bullet casing in the driveway—an indentation in the home's siding told him that a bullet had pierced the wall and traveled outside.

Approaching the back door, he peered in and saw Kewaii's body. Inside, everyone in the house was frozen in horror.

CHAPTER 3

A PROSECUTOR CALLED TO ACTION

THAT EVENING, I HAD BEEN serving as toastmaster at Mount Carmel Church's annual dinner in Pittston—a hall filled with friends and community leaders. I loved these kinds of events. They were uniquely Pittston.

The crowd laughed at my jokes, so I quit while I was ahead and slipped out early.

When I got home, I found my wife, Nicole, and our then two-year-old son, Dominick, cuddled on the couch. I ran upstairs, changed into a T-shirt and sweats, and lay down next to them, trying not to disturb them too much.

After 10 p.m., my phone started buzzing on the table. It was Luzerne County chief detective Michael Dessoye.

Mike calls me only when someone is killed.

I answered.

"We have a woman killed at 134 Lehigh Street in Wilkes-Barre," he said. "Get your ass down there."

"On my way," I said.

I changed and kissed Nicole and Dominick goodbye. Nicole was getting used to my running off at all hours, chasing killers. I sped toward Wilkes-Barre with my mind racing. My Sunday night was over, and it was time to focus.

When I arrived at the scene, I stood in that house and felt the weight of it all.

This was a home that should have been filled with warmth, not violence. I looked at the broken laundry basket, the couch, and thought, *This is what a Sunday night should have been.*

A mother doing laundry and some errands for the coming week.

Children watching a movie.

Not this.

Blood was all over the walls and ceiling—even on the ceiling fan propeller. Even now, when I close my eyes, I can still see it.

I left the scene and spent the rest of the night at Wilkes-Barre police headquarters, typing up warrants with detectives, reverse-engineering the Buckners' lives. Officers conducted interviews and searched for Donnell Buckner everywhere.

Police detectives found him the next day, on top of the abandoned Great Northern Press building, muttering about suicide. He was wearing a striped shirt, later found to contain Kewaii's blood spatter.

"I'm surprised you found me so fast," he told the detectives.

The building was so unstable that police had to use a ladder from a fire truck to bring him down.

Victim advocates arranged for the children to eventually be taken to their grandmother, Kim Rogers, in Mississippi. The family dog was left behind and had to be sheltered. A small group of victim advocates arranged for and funded the dog's return to Mississippi to be reunited with the kids. A glimmer of light in the darkness.

CHAPTER 4

BRINGING DONNELL BUCKNER TO JUSTICE

THE CASE MOVED SLOWLY. AFTER a brief preliminary hearing, the trial was looming. I had made inquiries to the defense attorneys regarding Donnell's intentions. I really did not offer much by way of a plea bargain. The trial was inevitable, and it eventually arrived in June 2010. We agreed to a bench trial (meaning a judge would rule on the case) in lieu of a jury trial. Judge Tina Gartley—a mother, a former prosecutor, and an advocate for victims of domestic violence—was set to preside over her first trial.

Donnell's defense hinged on a claim of temporary insanity, a desperate attempt to chip away at the prosecution's case for first-degree murder. Psychiatrists also diagnosed Buckner with bipolar disorder and depression. The defense suspected that a judge might be more inclined to accept this type of defense than a jury would.

When Donnell took the stand, he tried to portray himself as a broken man who had lost control. He started crying during his testimony, trying to sell his story with tears.

I wasn't buying it. I didn't want the court to buy it either.

As my cross-examination was about to begin, my co-counsel, Assistant District Attorney Frank McCabe, jokingly whispered to me, pointing to tissues on our table, "Bring him a tissue."

I said, "You know what, watch this."

I walked quickly toward Donnell on the witness stand, a box of tissues in hand. I slammed it down on the stand in front of him. I said, "You're going to need these."

I moved in close—close enough for him to know I wasn't afraid. Close enough to smell him.

This wasn't theatrics. It was about control. Donnell wasn't in charge anymore.

And it worked. He faltered. The man who had once terrorized his family suddenly seemed small. Powerless.

The most powerful testimony came from their twelve-year-old daughter. I won't name her to protect her.

Preparing her was one of the hardest things I've ever done. How do you ask a child to re-live the worst night of their life?

When it was time for her to testify, I announced her name in open court and we could hear her wailing through the thick wooden doors from the hallway outside.

I took a deep breath.

Judge Gartley's chin trembled as she listened.

But Kewaii's daughter, like her mother had been, was brave.

"When you're on that stand," I'd told her, "it's just you and me talking." I had spent many days preparing with her. I wanted her to be comfortable with me so it would ease some of her pain.

When the moment came, she walked into that courtroom with her head held high and took her seat before the court and a crowded courtroom. When it came time, and I asked her, "Who killed your mother?" she pointed at Donnell.

"That's him," she said.

Her strength was a testament to the kind of mother Kewaii had been.

The trial lasted all week, each day filled with heart-wrenching testimony and damning evidence. We brought in forensic experts, who detailed the trajectory of the bullets; medical examiners, who described the extent of Kewaii's injuries; and our own psychiatrists, who dismantled Donnell's insanity defense, including Dr. John O'Brien, a trained attorney and world-class psychiatrist.

We reached closing arguments before the judge. First, I reminded the judge that she had heard Dr. Mary Pascucci, the pathologist, testify that the first gunshot had been a distant shot. Despite the defense counsel's objection, we heard the doctor confirm that it had been the first shot.

I asked, "Well, how do we know it was the first shot?" Dr. Pascucci explained that Kewaii could not have survived the second or third shots. So, we have this first gunshot—she was protecting her face. It was distant because there was no soot, no burning, no stippling.

What happened next? No resolution. No dropping the PFA. Kewaii continued to beg for her life.

Donnell could have turned around and walked away. But what did he do?

Here's a paraphrasing of my closing statements:

He didn't walk away, Judge. He moved in closer. He made it more personal. He shot her not once but twice in the head—he put two holes in her skull and splattered her brains all over that house. That is exactly what he did.

Just like he said he was going to do, Judge.

And here's where the train goes off the tracks. He did it in front of their children. Again—not the first time.

You know why, Judge? Because that's the ultimate act of control. This is a man who was emasculated by her parenting ability, by her education, by her ability to work and raise those babies. And in one final act, he showed everyone who was in charge. That's what he did.

Judge, can you conceive of anything in your life—anything—worse than witnessing your own mother's execution at the hands of your father?

We heard the 911 recording from inside 134 Lehigh Street that night. We couldn't believe it, but we heard it. We heard their daughter describe what he was wearing—a black sweatshirt caked in Kewaii's blood. That alone tells you how personal this was. He was practically on top of her when he shot her. The jeans, the striped shirt—all of it covered in her blood. And we heard it from our experts. We know whose DNA was on that clothing. He was there, and those were the clothes he wore.

Now let's talk about his intention.

To find the defendant guilty of third-degree murder is to ignore everything we know about domestic violence. We know it's not an isolated episode. We know it follows a pattern—an escalating pattern. And we know the most dangerous time for a victim is at the moment of separation.

The PFA. That was the separation. That was the moment he had to turn up the heat. And he knew it.

Kewaii Rogers lived her life in a constant state of fear—under siege by this man. His intention didn't start that night. It began long ago when he set out on a course of abuse. His threats became knives. Knives became guns. And ultimately, those guns became murder.

That's what happened here, Judge. That's exactly what happened.

And then he takes the stand, crying crocodile tears, claiming how sorry he is. But he isn't sorry for what he did. He's sorry for himself.

Because what other story could he tell? What else could he say other than, "I don't remember what happened"?

Her blood was all over him. He left eyewitnesses—his own children.

And now, Judge, we are left with a decision. A decision I know you do not take lightly.

We are left to pick up the pieces.

Mr. Buckner sits before you, awaiting your judgment.

Kewaii will never see her children grow up.

We never got to meet her, but the apple doesn't fall far from the tree. One of the hardest moments I've ever faced in this job was hearing that child wail in the hallway when you called her to the stand.

Do you want to know who Kewaii was? Look at her daughter. She was beautiful. She was smart. And she wasn't afraid of him.

But now it's too late. It's too late to save her. It's too late to erase this nightmare from those children's memories. It's too late to enforce the PFA.

But it is not too late for justice. Justice, in this case, demands the highest penalty.

This man's cruelty is an anomaly. I repeat—an anomaly.

We need a decision that provides our community with the greatest protection. We know what a first-degree murder conviction carries. And I'm not interested in caricatures.

Is this an evil man? It doesn't matter. What matters is that he is a man hell-bent on achieving control. And he will do whatever it takes to get what he wants.

Judge, we ask for justice. We ask for a conviction of first-degree murder. For the murder of Kewaii Rogers Buckner.

A mother of three. A daughter. A sister. A citizen of our community.

And she deserves justice. Yes, she deserves justice.

My closing statement wasn't just about proving Donnell's guilt. It was about showing the court who Kewaii had been. During my closing, I said, "We don't get to know Kewaii anymore. But if you want to see who she was, look at her daughter. Look at her bravery, her strength. That's Kewaii's legacy." I said it and it reminded me of my own mother. In my heart, I knew that I was the product of a mother who sacrificed like Kewaii. My mother was the product of Grammy, who did the same for her. Donnell Buckner took all that away. That's what crushed me about this case. The world outside wasn't tough enough but Kewaii's danger was on the inside too.

CHAPTER 5

GRACE IN THE FACE OF EVIL

BUCKNER WAS REPRESENTED BY ATTORNEYS William Ruzzo and Mark Singer. Both counsel were capable lawyers and prepared. They attempted to argue the blackout defense, and that this was not a preplanned killing. The case was not a whodunnit. It was an effort to negate the level of intention and perhaps allow for Buckner to be found guilty of a lesser degree of murder.

Judge Gartley handed down a guilty verdict of first-degree murder. I felt a sense of relief but also sadness. No verdict could bring Kewaii back. Buckner would be automatically sentenced to life without the possibility of parole.

The sentencing hearing was next, and that's when Kim Rogers, Kewaii's mother, delivered another moment that would stay with me forever. Even though Buckner's fate of life was automatic. Victims are given the opportunity to be heard. I came to know Kim as the case was pending. She was always patient with our team and lovingly accepted the responsibility of raising Kewaii's children.

She stood in that courtroom, facing the man who had destroyed her family. "I forgive you," she said. "I have no hate for you. I only have love in my heart for you."

I felt like a forgiveness bomb had gone off. I was in proximity to the blast and it was an incredible experience. The room fell silent. Her words weren't just about forgiveness; they were about reclaiming power. Donnell deflated at that moment. You could see it. Kim's grace had stripped him of the control he so desperately clung to.

Forgiveness is a concept I thought I understood. I had grown up in Catholic schools and attended church regularly, but that moment taught me more about forgiveness than any sermon ever could.

Kim Rogers, another amazing mother, showed me that forgiveness isn't about excusing the inexcusable. It's about freeing yourself from the anger and hatred that can consume you.

This case taught me about courage—the courage to seek help, to face your fears, to stand up to evil. It taught me about resilience—the kind that lets a mother's legacy live on in her children. And it taught me about the transformative power of forgiveness.

CHAPTER 6

HER LEGACY LIVES ON

KEWAII'S STORY IS ONE OF strength in the face of unimaginable hardship. Her daughter's bravery and her mother's grace remind us that even in the darkest moments, light can shine through.

For anyone reading this, let Kewaii's life and legacy serve as a reminder: strength isn't about just standing up to your fears; it's about finding the grace to rise above them.

As the case ended, I found myself reflecting deeply on the weight of the justice system and the lives it touches. The courtroom isn't a place just for verdicts; it's a crucible where truth, pain, and redemption collide.

It's a place where stories like Kewaii's, though tragic, can inspire profound change. This wasn't just a victory for the prosecution—it was a testament to what's possible when we refuse to let fear dictate our actions.

For Donnell Buckner, life in prison was his sentence, but for those he left in his wake, life continued. Kewaii's children, under the loving care of their grandmother, began to heal.

The memory of their mother lives on in their laughter, their resilience, and their determination to build lives that Kewaii would have been proud of. And for me, every step of this case reaffirmed why I do what I do.

It reminded me that justice is often about giving a voice to the voiceless, about standing with the victims and showing the world that their lives matter.

Kewaii's story, her courage, and her legacy will remain with me forever. Her strength reminds us all that even in the face of unimaginable darkness, we have the power to rise, to forgive, and to carry forward the light of those we've lost.

To truly understand the gravity of the trial, consider the emotional toll it took on everyone involved. The witnesses, many of them friends and family, relived their darkest memories on the stand. Detectives recounted their first moments at the scene, describing the horror they faced.

Psychiatrists debated Donnell Buckner's mental state with fervor, turning the courtroom into an intellectual battlefield. Every moment was charged, and every word carried weight.

This trial was a microcosm of humanity—its potential for cruelty and its capacity for resilience. The days were long, filled with heartbreak and hope. And through it all, the lesson was clear: justice is a legal and moral concept.

Kewaii's case reminded us all of the importance of standing up, speaking out, and refusing to let fear win. Her story belongs to all of us, a testament to the human spirit's ability to endure, forgive, and transcend.

LESSONS IN MOTIVATION: FORGIVENESS AS A PATH TO PERSONAL LIBERATION

Forgiveness is one of the most profound acts of humanity, and yet it's often misunderstood. It's easy to think of forgiveness as a concession, a sign of weakness, or a way of excusing an injustice.

But in the courtroom where I saw Kim Rogers forgive her daughter's murderer, I learned that forgiveness is none of those things. It is power—an active and deliberate choice to rise above anger, hatred, and the instinct for revenge. It is a tool of healing and motivation, both for the forgiver and the forgiven.

In the case of Donnell Buckner, forgiveness became a transformative force. When Kim stood in that courtroom and said, "I forgive you," she reclaimed control over her life and her emotions. In that moment, forgiveness wasn't about Donnell's actions; it was about Kim's ability to release herself from the destructive power of anger and grief. It was about showing her family, her grandchildren, and the world that love and grace could triumph over hatred.

So, what can we learn from this extraordinary act of forgiveness? How can we use it to motivate ourselves and others to move forward in the face of pain, betrayal, and loss? The lessons are as deep as they are universal.

Forgiveness is not about letting someone off the hook; it's about freeing yourself from the chains of resentment. Kim Rogers could have stood in that courtroom and unleashed her anger at Donnell. I wouldn't have blamed her; I expected it. She would have been justified in doing so. But what would that have achieved? Her anger wouldn't have changed the past, and it wouldn't have brought Kewaii back. Instead, it would have kept her tethered to the pain and bitterness that had already consumed so much of her life.

By forgiving Donnell, Kim chose a different path. She chose to release herself from the burden of anger. She chose to focus on healing, both for herself and her grandchildren. This is a lesson for all of us. When we forgive, we don't erase the past, but we stop letting it define our future. We take back our power, our peace, and our ability to live fully.

Forgiveness as a Model for Others

Forgiveness is contagious. When Kim forgave Donnell, she set an example for her grandchildren and for everyone in that courtroom. She showed them that even in the face of unimaginable pain, it's possible to choose grace. For her grandchildren, this act of forgiveness became a guiding light, a reminder that they could rise above their circumstances and carry forward their mother's legacy of strength and love.

As leaders, parents, or simply members of a community, we all have the power to model forgiveness. When we forgive, we show others that it's possible to move forward without bitterness. We demonstrate that forgiveness is not a sign of weakness but of incredible strength. It's a message that can inspire those around us to find their own paths to healing.

Forgiveness as a Tool for Growth

Forgiveness is a process. It requires introspection, courage, and a willingness to confront our own pain. For Kim, forgiving Donnell wasn't about excusing his actions. It was about acknowledging her own pain and choosing not to let it consume her. It was about growing beyond the tragedy that had defined her life.

This process of forgiveness can be deeply motivational. It forces us to look inward, to understand our emotions, and to take control of our lives. In doing so, we become stronger, more resilient, and more capable of facing future challenges. Forgiveness doesn't just heal the past; it prepares us for the future.

The Ripple Effect of Forgiveness

When Kim forgave Donnell, the impact went beyond her own healing. It affected everyone in that courtroom. Even Donnell, who had spent his life exerting control through fear and violence, was visibly shaken. Kim's forgiveness stripped him of his power. It was a reminder that love and grace are stronger than hatred and violence.

The ripple effect of forgiveness can be profound. When we forgive, we create a ripple of positivity that can extend to our families, communities, and even strangers. We break the cycle of anger and retaliation, replacing it with compassion and understanding. This ripple effect can motivate others to forgive, to heal, and to build stronger, more connected communities.

Forgiveness and Leadership

Leadership often requires us to make difficult choices, to rise above our emotions, and to act in the best interests of those we serve. Kim's act of forgiveness was a powerful example of leadership. She showed her grandchildren and her community that it's possible to choose love over hate, even in the most trying circumstances. She showed them that true leadership is about inspiring others to be their best selves.

We all can learn from Kim's example. Forgiveness is not just a personal act; it's a leadership tool. It's a way to create a culture of compassion, understanding, and resilience. When we forgive, we lead by example, showing others that it's possible to overcome adversity with grace and strength.

Forgiveness as a Source of Motivation

One of the most powerful benefits of forgiveness is its ability to motivate us to live better, fuller lives. For Kim, forgiveness wasn't just about healing; it was about honoring Kewaii's memory. By forgiving Donnell, she chose to focus on the positive aspects of Kewaii's life—her love, her strength, her legacy—rather than the tragedy of her death.

This is a lesson for all of us. When we forgive, we shift our focus from what we've lost to what we still have. We find motivation in the memories of those we've lost, in the relationships we still cherish, and in the goals we still want to achieve. Forgiveness allows us to move forward with purpose and determination.

Practical Steps to Embrace Forgiveness

Forgiveness, as I said earlier, is a journey, and it's not always an easy one. Here are some steps to help you embrace forgiveness and use it as a source of motivation:

Acknowledge Your Pain: Before you can forgive, you need to confront your emotions. Acknowledge the hurt, anger, and grief you're feeling. Give yourself permission to feel those emotions without judgment.

Understand Forgiveness: Forgiveness doesn't mean condoning the actions that hurt you. It means choosing not to let those actions control your life. It's about freeing yourself, not the person who hurt you.

Find Meaning in the Experience: Look for lessons in the pain. How has this experience shaped you? What have you learned about yourself, others, or life in general?

Seek Support: Forgiveness is a deeply personal journey, but that doesn't mean you have to do it alone. Seek support from friends, family, or a counselor. Share your feelings and lean on others for strength.

Take Your Time: Forgiveness is not instant, not a destination. Be patient with yourself. Give yourself the time and space you need to heal.

Choose Forgiveness Daily: Forgiveness is not a one-time act; it's a daily choice. Each day, remind yourself of your decision to let go of anger and focus on healing.

The Power of Forgiveness in Our Lives

Kim Rogers' act of forgiveness in the courtroom was a shining example of this power. It was a reminder that even in the face of unimaginable pain, we have the ability to choose love, grace, and resilience.

Her story inspires us all to embrace forgiveness, not as a weakness but as one of the greatest strengths we can possess.

Wendy Cadwalader and her sister, Micayla Grey, visit the grave of Carrie Martin (2010, courtesy of The Citizens' Voice*).*

Preparing Paul Weakley to testify in the Hugo Selenski trial. Also pictured is Det. Chaz Balogh and Pennsylvania State Trooper Steve Polishan (2015).

The Hugo Selenski Trial Team. Standing: (then) Detective Gary "Cap" Capitano, Detective Daniel Yursha, Pennsylvania State Trooper Steve Polishan. Seated: (then) Assistant District Attorneys Luke Moran, Mamie Phillips, and Jarrett Ferentino; Geri Kerkowski; District Attorney Stefanie Salavantis; First Assistant District Attorney Sam Sanguedolce (2015).

Holding a press conference after a homicide case with (then) Assistant District Attorneys Gary Scott and Brittany Quinn, and Pennsylvania State Trooper Edward Urban (2020).

Walking into court during the Selenski trial (2015).

Nicole, Dominick, and Victoria visiting Dad at the Luzerne County Courthouse (2021).

Kim Rogers, mother of Kewaii Rogers Buckner (2024).

Brittanee Drexel, prior to her disappearance (2009).

Jarrett Ferentino with his daughter, Victoria, working out and trial-prepping (2015).

Dawn Drexel and Jarrett Ferentino (2022, courtesy of The Post and Courier*).*

Jarrett Ferentino and his mother, Rose (2025).

Swearing in as an Assistant District Attorney with (then) District Attorney David W. Lupas and First Assistant Jackie Musto Carroll (2004).

Nicole, Jarrett, Victoria, and Dominick Ferentino (2025).

Friday, February 13, 2015 Newsstand 50¢

DEAL OF THE DAY » $20 FOR $10 AT LIZZA'S MEZZO MEZZO: Page 2

PIPELINE FOCUS OF MEETING
Some opposed to PennEast proposal
IMPACT HEARING: PAGE 5

MERCURY TAKES A PLUNGE
Potentially dangerous temperatures on tap
CHILLY NEPA: PAGE 3

HOOPS SQUADS EYE PRIZE
Holy Redeemer, GAR win division titles
DIVISION 2, 3: PAGE 28

The prosecution team escorts Geraldine Kerkowski, Michael Kerkowski's mother, second from left, and Lisa Sands, Tammy Fassett's sister, third from left, from the courthouse Wednesday night.

SWEET RELIEF

For families, Selenski verdict turned hopes into reality. Page 4

BREAKING NEWS, BLOGS, VIDEOS & MORE AT CITIZENSVOICE.COM
LIKE THE CITIZENS' VOICE ON FACEBOOK AND FOLLOW @CITIZENSVOICE ON TWITTER

WB_VOICE - DLY - 1 - 02/13/15 WB_VOICE/PAGES [T01] | 02/12/15 22:42 | LOPERAIAN

The cover of The Citizens' Voice, February 13, 2015: Jarrett Ferentino holding the hand of Mrs. Geri Kerkowski as they exit the courthouse following the guilty verdict of Hugo Selenski. Also pictured are (then) District Attorney Salavantis and First Assistant District Attorney Sanguedolce (2015, courtesy of The Citizens' Voice).

Hugo Selenski led to his arraignment on homicide charges (2002, courtesy of The Citizens' Voice).

Tiffany Simmons is led into her preliminary hearing for the prosecution in the death of her three-month-old child, Xavier Simmons (2008, courtesy of The Citizens' Voice).

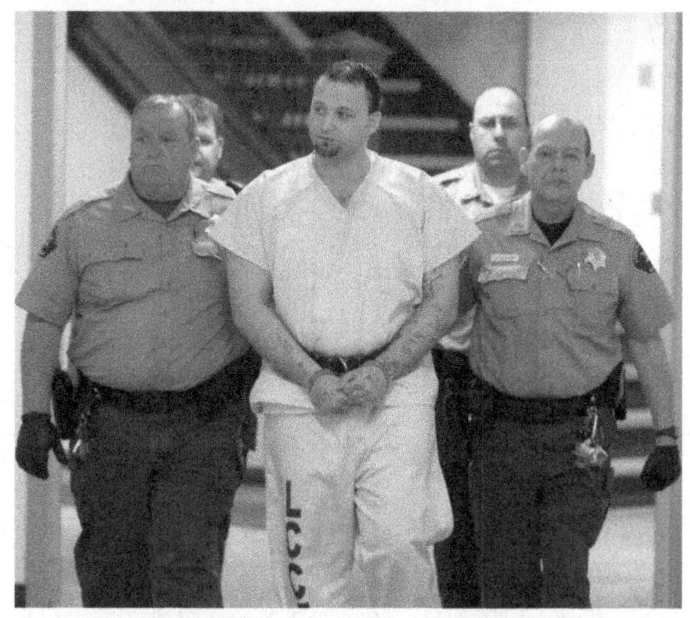

Alan Lietzel is led to a court proceeding for the murder of three-month-old Xavier Simmons (2009, courtesy of The Citizens' Voice).

Joseph Gacha exits the courthouse following his conviction of first-degree murder in the death of Luzerne County Fair Queen Carrie Lynn Martin (2006, courtesy of The Citizens' Voice).

Kewaii Rogers Buckner, murder victim at the hands of her estranged husband, Donnell Buckner (2009, courtesy of The Citizens' Voice).

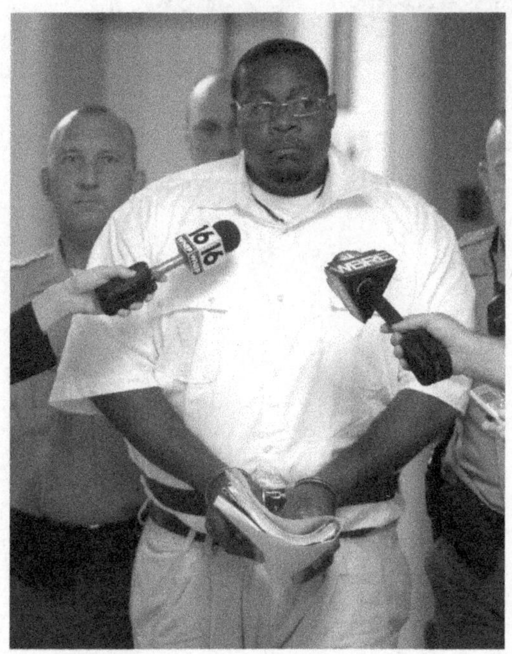

Donnell Buckner is escorted to court (2009).

Carrie Lynn Martin, senior year of high school (2003).

Book 3

THE BABY WHO COULD HAVE BEEN PRESIDENT

Commonwealth v. Tiffany Simmons and Alan Leitzel

"The ones who have a voice must speak for those who are voiceless."

—St. Óscar Romero, Patron Saint of Persecuted Christians

CHAPTER 1

"YOU WILL NEVER SLEEP ANOTHER PEACEFUL NIGHT"

MY WIFE'S GRANDMOTHER, MARY BOSCO, was a sweet and kind soul.

Coincidentally, Mary worked in the same dress factory as my own grandmother—the Lee Manufacturing Dress Factory in Pittston, Pennsylvania. These women worked on their feet every day, pressing clothing in some of the harshest conditions.

And just like my mother and grandmother, Mary had a huge influence on my wife and, in the case described below, on me as a prosecutor.

In October 2006, Mary was holding Dominick for the first time at the hospital shortly after he was born. She cried with joy and said he was so beautiful. She said something to us that I never forgot: "You will never sleep another peaceful night."

She then added, "But that's OK, because that's the way it's supposed to be."

We smiled, accepted, and acknowledged our fate as new parents.

In those years, my three brothers and I all had married and were starting our own families. It felt like a new baby showed up weekly at my mother's house for Sunday dinner.

Being a father and an uncle was special to me. I was crazy about all of the kids and their emerging personalities. Mary's words stuck with me when I was assigned my next case, which included the murder of an infant.

Mary's advice began to torment me in this case. Never sleeping a peaceful night was for Mary an ideal, and in this case became the judge and jury.

I thought about how she, my mother, and my grandmothers had sacrificed all for their children. They'd spent their days and nights ensuring their babies were safe, not pursuing their own pleasure and enjoyment. I was about to learn that not all mothers put their children above their own pursuits and the deadly consequences that can follow.

CHAPTER 2

A FRAGILE LIFE AT RISK

ON OCTOBER 10, 2007, XAVIER Elliott Simmons was born—one year after my own son. Xavier was born to Tiffany Simmons and was her fourth child.

Over the course of the next several weeks, Tiffany would lose custody of three of her children following an accusation by their father and paternal aunt that she and her new boyfriend, Alan Leitzel, were using heroin.

On December 11, 2007, Luzerne County Children and Youth Services officials held a meeting with Tiffany regarding the custodial status of her children. During that meeting, she acknowledged that she had had a physically violent altercation with Leitzel in the presence of her children. Following the meeting, officials granted custody of three of her children to their biological father.

Baby Xavier was the only child who remained in Tiffany's custody, as he had a different biological father, who was incarcerated. Tiffany agreed that she would ensure that Xavier would have absolutely no contact whatsoever with Leitzel.

Officials told Tiffany that if Xavier were to have contact with Leitzel, she would face legal action and consequences. She entered into a written safety plan acknowledging that Xavier would have no contact with Leitzel.

Despite these restrictions and known red flags regarding Leitzel, Tiffany began to visit Leitzel with Xavier at the residence of one of her female friends in West Hazleton.

On December 27, 2007, Children and Youth Services followed up on continued reports that Tiffany was bringing Xavier to a residence with Leitzel. When interviewed, Tiffany denied these allegations. The reports were deemed unfounded, and Xavier remained with Tiffany, subject to the safety plan.

On January 14, 2008, at 7 a.m., Tiffany arrived with three-month-old Xavier at the emergency room at Hazleton General Hospital. Upon arrival, Xavier had no pulse and wasn't breathing.

Xavier was in grave danger. Emergency medical personnel were able to reestablish his pulse, as well as limited respiration, with the assistance of a respirator. Doctors determined that he must be transferred via ambulance to the Lehigh Valley Hospital Center near Allentown for advanced life-saving treatment, and he arrived there at approximately 10 a.m.

He was treated in the pediatric intensive care unit by Dr. Kerrie Pinkney, a pediatric intensivist. Dr. Pinkney found that Xavier's body temperature was extremely low, and his pupils were fixed and dilated.

These were indications of a severe brain injury. Subsequent tests confirmed that Xavier had absolutely no brain activity. Dr. Pinkney had seen this before. This was not a natural process; someone had hurt Xavier, and he was dying.

The hospital contacted the Pennsylvania State Police and informed them that Xavier was exhibiting signs of nonaccidental head trauma consistent with being shaken. The Pennsylvania State Police swept into action and traveled to the Lehigh Valley Hospital.

Police interviewed Tiffany at the Lehigh Valley Hospital. She explained that she and Xavier had been staying at the residence of a female friend located on Bator Street in West Hazleton.

She initially claimed that she had been alone with Xavier in a bedroom. She said that she fed Xavier around 5:30 a.m., and that she awoke around 7 a.m. and heard Xavier making a choking sound. When she went to Xavier, she found that he had vomit around his nose and mouth.

She described Xavier as being limp and said she tried to remove the vomit with a suction bulb.

Tiffany told investigators that she then yelled for help. She and her female friend then took Xavier to Hazleton General Hospital.

Investigators pressed Tiffany, noting that her account did not add up and did not comport with the medical professionals' assessment of Xavier.

As the interview continued, and investigators confronted Tiffany with her inconsistencies, she admitted that she was not being completely truthful about the incident but didn't want to point fingers at anyone.

She then told investigators that her boyfriend, Alan Leitzel, also had been present in the home and bedroom.

CHAPTER 3

CONFESSIONS, RACISM, AND REMORSELESSNESS

TIFFANY STATED THAT SHE HAD fed Xavier at 5:30 a.m. and that he'd been fine. She said she then fell asleep, and about an hour later, Leitzel awakened her, screaming her name and holding Xavier.

Tiffany said that Xavier was limp and unresponsive, that she attempted CPR but was unsuccessful. She stated that she then took him to the hospital.

Investigators learned about the safety plan that prohibited Xavier from being in the presence of Leitzel. They asked Tiffany about it.

This is where things went from bad to much worse.

She acknowledged that she had agreed to the safety plan and admitted that Children and Youth Services had cautioned her because Leitzel had a "bad temper."

She then told investigators that Leitzel had major issues with the fact that Xavier was biracial. Tiffany said that Leitzel had referred to Xavier as an "[N-word] baby" and had called her an "[N-word] lover."

Tiffany said that Leitzel had struck her in the past, resulting in a cut above her eye that required stitches. Despite her past experience of violence with Leitzel and warnings from Children and Youth Services, she'd continued to date him and allowed Xavier in his presence.

Tiffany admitted that she'd lied to Children and Youth Services when asked about the allegation that Xavier had been in the presence of Leitzel over the Christmas holiday, so that she could continue to go to her friend's house and be with Leitzel.

She also admitted that Leitzel would "bitch" to her about Xavier crying. She said that she never, however, saw Leitzel hurt or attempt to hurt Xavier.

Investigators learned that Leitzel did not accompany Simmons to Hazleton General Hospital when Xavier was taken there in the ambulance. Xavier was then set to be transported via ambulance to Lehigh Valley but Tiffany didn't ride down with Xavier. She went back to the Bator Street home to change, and Leitzel traveled with her to Lehigh Valley. Tiffany indicated that while traveling down to the Lehigh Valley Hospital, Leitzel never told her that he had shaken Xavier or hurt him in any way.

Investigators had already learned that Leitzel quickly left the Lehigh Valley Hospital while Xavier was being treated. Now they asked Tiffany if he had told her where he was going, and she replied that she had not been aware that he had gone. Tiffany explained that after speaking with Dr. Pinkney, she left the room only to learn that Leitzel was already gone.

Despite the best efforts of all the doctors and the rest of the medical team, Xavier died as a result of his injuries. This beautiful little boy had been in this world for only three months.

Leitzel left the hospital and lay low for a bit in the McAdoo area outside of Hazleton. On January 15, 2008, police eventually caught up with him and brought him in for questioning.

He was read his Miranda rights and signed a form acknowledging that he understood his rights. Leitzel said he had known Tiffany since they were younger. He said they'd started dating about two months earlier, while he was still incarcerated at the Luzerne County Prison.

A few days after he was released from jail, Tiffany began living at her friend's house. Shortly thereafter, she would bring Xavier to the home and eventually for overnight stays. Leitzel was staying there with them.

Leitzel began to speak about the events that occurred on the morning of January 14, 2008. He said he'd been awakened sometime after 5 a.m. because Xavier was fussing in the bassinet. When he heard Xavier crying, he attempted to wake Tiffany, but she didn't get up.

Leitzel said that he then reached down and removed Xavier from the bassinet. As he grabbed Xavier, he brought him up quickly and banged Xavier's head on the bassinet's plastic cover. Xavier immediately started crying.

Leitzel said he was growing angrier at Tiffany because he had been taking care of Xavier for the previous few nights. After hitting the baby's head on the bassinet cover, he tried to quiet Xavier down.

He said that approximately three minutes passed, and then Xavier closed his eyes. Leitzel put him back in the bassinet, then went downstairs to get a cigarette but couldn't locate one.

Leitzel told investigators that he returned to the bedroom, noticed Tiffany's cigarettes near the side of the bed, and lit one. At that point, he heard Xavier gasping for air. He picked up Xavier and screamed for Tiffany to wake up so she could take care of him.

While he attempted to wake Tiffany, he was holding Xavier in one arm and shaking Tiffany with the other. He said that he was very angry because she wouldn't get up. Leitzel related that while he was looking at Tiffany, he shook the baby back and forth two or three times while yelling at her.

When asked how he shook Xavier, Leitzel raised his arms and indicated that he'd had Xavier around the chest, not supporting his head, and shaken him back and forth. He demonstrated the shaking using one of the investigator's notebooks.

Leitzel couldn't say whether Xavier's head was snapping back and forth, because he was so angry at the time; he'd been looking at Tiffany, not Xavier.

After shaking Xavier and attempting to wake Tiffany, he noticed the baby had gone limp. He began screaming for help. Tiffany finally woke up. She attempted CPR but was unsuccessful. Tiffany then called an ambulance, which took Xavier to the hospital.

Leitzel said he remained at the house while Tiffany went to the hospital. She returned and told him that Xavier had been taken to Lehigh Valley, and that he traveled there with her. However, he did not stay there long.

Leitzel left the Lehigh Valley Hospital before the police could make contact with him. He explained that his friend drove him to Subway in West Hazleton and then dropped him off at a friend's house in McAdoo. Leitzel admitted that he had anger problems.

Investigators asked Leitzel if he'd used any racial epithets when talking about or interacting with Xavier. He admitted that he had called Xavier a "Moolinyan" and snickered, saying "it" was just an "eggplant to the investigators' disbelief."

Leitzel said that he had a dislike for "[N-word] s," was "[anti-N-word]," and "hates them Black people." He went on to say that he had called Xavier an "[N-word]" or an "[N-let]" in the past. However, he claimed he was only repeating words he had heard Tiffany use. He claimed he'd heard Tiffany call Xavier a "little asshole."

Investigators then informed Leitzel that Xavier had passed away. He had no reaction or expression of remorse upon learning this.

Leitzel further discussed his relationship with Tiffany and said he believed they would get married someday. However, his entire demeanor changed when investigators informed him that Tiffany had told them she had fed Xavier the day of the incident.

Leitzel became loud and very demonstrative. He said, "She didn't feed him. I fed him." He stated, "You should punch that bitch right in the mouth. She's a fucking liar."

He then reiterated what he'd told officers.

When asked where his rage stemmed from, Leitzel said the police needed to keep Tiffany and her mother away from him or he would kill them. He was upset because he felt Tiffany was placing the blame on him but that she had been the person responsible for Xavier.

Leitzel was arrested, charged, and jailed for the murder of Xavier.

CHAPTER 4

FEAR, FRIENDSHIP, AND THE WEIGHT OF JUSTICE

WHEN THE PENNSYLVANIA STATE POLICE became involved, and Detective Lieutenant Gary Capitano ("Cap") from the Luzerne County District Attorney's Office became our office's primary investigator, District Attorney Jackie Musto-Carroll assigned me to the case.

I loved Cap. He was a Citadel graduate, a former analyst at the FBI, and a self-described hard-ass Sicilian. Tough exterior but a big kid on the inside. I had recently begun working with him on the case of accused serial killer Hugo Selenski, one of the office's biggest cases in decades (more details to come!).

In addition to Gary, Jackie assigned Assistant District Attorney Dave Pedri as my co-counsel. Dave was my partner in the District Attorney's Office, another justice advocate with an eye toward bigger things. He was also a new father and a very capable prosecutor.

Dave remains one of my closest friends and confidants. I was never afraid to think out loud with him and even discuss my vulnerabilities and fears in our work together.

I was confident that I had a great team that was going to work for justice for baby Xavier. But I was also afraid. I had never prosecuted a baby murder before, and I knew it would require special skills and extensive medical testimony.

So, I buckled down and read what I could about shaken baby syndrome and nonaccidental trauma to children. I remember that as I pored over the reports, I read about how Tiffany wouldn't wake up as Leitzel screamed at her and was killing Xavier in the same room.

I thought about Mary's forewarning that as a parent, you won't ever sleep a peaceful night. Yet Tiffany slept peacefully as Leitzel yelled at her and shook and slammed Xavier.

I wanted to be able to speak the medical language when I met with our experts, and I wanted to understand what happens in cases like this and how a case like this can happen. We weren't comfortable charging only Leitzel; We believed that Tiffany should be held accountable as well.

We charged Tiffany with the involuntary manslaughter of Xavier. Essentially, we alleged that she had recklessly disregarded a risk to Xavier that led to his death.

We also charged her with endangering the welfare of a child. The endangering charge would be enhanced if we could prove that the endangerment wasn't a one-off but part of a course of conduct of endangering behaviors. When I learned of the safety plan, I thought that would be my hook.

The safety plan was a written warning—a contract, if you will—between Tiffany Simmons and Luzerne County. She acknowledged in one sense that Alan Leitzel was extremely dangerous and posed a danger to baby Xavier.

I knew that if I could show she had breached that contract and that the death of Xavier had resulted or potentially resulted from that breach, I would be able to establish that she had committed involuntary manslaughter.

Law school prepares you for the practice of law, but nothing prepares you to see a dead child, to see a mother who put her own interests ahead of that child, and to see people capable of such violence, disregard for human life, and complete lack of remorse.

Unfortunately, as a prosecutor, you become accustomed to these types of situations. But I'd be lying if I said I wasn't feeling overwhelmed.

In the prosecution business, fear and overwhelming cases can be your friend. They keep you sharp. They keep you preparing. They keep you on your toes.

I wanted to prove to Jackie Musto-Carroll and Cap that I could handle this case as the lead, even when the theory behind the charges was not as straightforward as for typical cases. I knew that having Dave Pedri with me would exponentially increase our chances of success.

CHAPTER 5

WHEN A MOTHER FAILS: THE STORY THAT SHOULD HAVE BEEN A BOY'S TO TELL

I BEGAN TO WORK UP the case. This moment was part of a deeper theme that seemed to recur throughout my entire career: what defines a mother, what sacrifice truly means, and how the absence of protection for a child reverberates across a community.

When a mother abandons her role, when the shield she is meant to be becomes a void, the system, and people like me, have to step in to fill that gap.

I've seen women rise from nothing, endure brutal hardship, and still show up for their kids with the strength of an entire army. I've also seen women turn their backs, failing in ways that leave a wake of pain and silence.

I've stood over a lot of bodies. Some were found under bridges, others in alleys or interred in shallow graves, the victims' final moments lost to bullets, blades, ropes...you name it.

But when I stepped into the autopsy room on January 15, 2008, and saw the broken little body of Xavier Simmons, I felt something shift in me.

This wasn't a gangland murder. It wasn't drugs or domestic revenge. This was an innocent baby, lifeless, fragile, and robbed of a story that had barely even begun.

At the time, as I said earlier, I was a new father myself. I knew the weight of a baby's head in my arms, the softness of his breath against my chest, the vulnerability that comes with complete dependence.

I used to wear the same soft sweatshirt when my son was that small. I wanted him to feel that familiar softness when he was in his father's arms. Xavier never knew that kind of softness in this world. At three months old, he was already in the Children and Youth Services system, bouncing between houses. He didn't know his father and was not a priority to his own mother.

Xavier was completely dependent, but no one protected him. His story would never be his to tell. So I had to tell it for him.

CHAPTER 6

A MOTHER'S DUTY AND THE LETTER THAT BROKE US

TIFFANY SIMMONS, AGE TWENTY-FIVE AT the time of the trial, was Xavier's biological mother. But that title, mother, comes with expectations, duties, legal obligations, and instinctual protections that she abandoned the moment she let her boyfriend Alan Leitzel into her son's life.

This wasn't an accident. This wasn't a lapse in judgment. This was part of a pattern of selfish neglect, a refusal to heed repeated warnings culminating in a betrayal so deep, it cost Xavier his life.

Attorney Shelley Centini, a young mother herself, represented Tiffany. Centini was no slouch. She was a fine lawyer and was earning a reputation as one of the best defense attorneys in the county.

She argued that Xavier's death had not been foreseeable from Tiffany's perspective. She claimed that charging Tiffany was an overreach. She argued that if it had been so crystal clear and foreseeable that Xavier could have been killed, then Children and Youth Services should have taken him from her.

I rebutted, saying that a plan for Xavier's safety had been in place, and it clearly said that Tiffany was not to have Xavier in the presence of Leitzel, for the baby's safety. This meant that Leitzel had posed a danger to Xavier.

I noted that every danger to a defenseless three-month-old is potentially mortal danger.

Tiffany's own mother, despite her personal struggles, was helping raise Tiffany's children. She described Tiffany as a "demon from hell." Social services had already been involved. Children and Youth Services had been supervising Tiffany's interactions with her children for some time, and when she began seeing Leitzel, a known criminal with a history of violent behavior, they stepped in.

The safety plan had been issued on December 11, 2007. It was clear. Simple. Xavier was not to be near Leitzel. An action item stated that Tiffany would ensure that Xavier would have no contact with Alan Leitzel and denoted Tiffany as the person responsible.

It was meant to be a lifeline. A legal shield for Xavier.

But Tiffany ignored it.

Tiffany wrote Leitzel a thirteen-page love letter just five weeks after Xavier was killed, while Leitzel was in jail and awaiting trial for killing Xavier. In it, she called Leitzel "baby." Promised him breakfast. Flirted and fantasized about their life after his release. But not once—not once—did she mention Xavier. The child he had killed. Her child.

I eventually read that letter to the jury. I remember saying, "You know why she didn't mention Xavier? Because she knew it would piss Alan off. Her loyalty wasn't to her son. It was to the man who took his life."

That was the moment we knew: Tiffany hadn't just failed her child; she had betrayed him.

She wasn't the one who had shaken Xavier, slammed him, fractured his skull. But she had laid the path. She had handed him over to the man who did.

Tiffany Simmons chose to protect Alan Leitzel instead of her own son. She did that in her actions and inactions. She did that in her omissions. She did that in her letters. She did that in her lies.

Tiffany wasn't writing to Alan about her son. She was calling Alan her baby, dreaming of him, planning for a future. Those words should have belonged to Xavier.

She'd had the power to protect, and she chose not to. That made her complicit.

And I wasn't going to let her hide behind excuses or some legal technicality.

CHAPTER 7

THE ANATOMY OF NOT LISTENING

XAVIER'S MURDER HAD BEEN PREVENTABLE.

The case put Luzerne County Children and Youth Services under scrutiny. A state investigation revealed that the agency had delayed removing Xavier from Tiffany Simmons' care, despite known risks.

The Department of Public Welfare determined that Simmons had broken the safety plan, which barred her from allowing contact between Xavier and Alan Leitzel. This failure led to the state's downgrading the agency's status to provisional until at least September 1, 2008.

The Department of Public Welfare's findings harshly criticized Children and Youth Services for not taking prompt action once it had become aware that Simmons had violated its directive.

If you're asking how this happened, you're not alone. Xavier died under the watch of not just a mother but an entire system.

Children and Youth Services had flagged Leitzel. There was a written safety plan. Social workers had visited. Parole agents had checked in. And yet, it wasn't enough.

We continued to prepare our case and move forward. I met the witnesses for the first time, meeting with the Children and Youth Services representatives.

In that meeting, they were apprehensive and fearful. I know they felt some responsibility and were heartbroken, but they were guarded in their responses to Dave and me.

I lost my cool a little bit and said, "Whatever you're worried about, you need to be upfront, because no matter what, system failure may have occurred here. A mother failed her child, and that's what this case is about. You cannot be consumed with any potential harm or liability to your office at the expense of justice for this little baby in criminal court."

I tried to be compassionate as well. I told them clearly that if they had known this was going to happen, they would have done something. They acknowledged my sentiment and began coming forward with the information.

Every time I replayed this case, I came back to the same question: What is the value of a warning if no one listens?

In my heart, I wanted to scream that the system had failed Xavier. But in the courtroom, I knew I had to prove that Tiffany had. That duality weighed heavily.

You can build policies. You can write plans. But if you don't have a parent who gives a damn, nothing holds.

CHAPTER 8

ANATOMY OF VIOLENCE: WHAT THE DOCTORS SAW

DR. SAMUEL LAND, WHO CONDUCTED Xavier's autopsy on January 17, 2008, determined that Xavier had died as a result of blunt force trauma to the head and torso. The baby had suffered a fractured skull and internal bleeding around the spinal cord, consistent with injuries caused by violent shaking.

I attended the autopsy. I stood at the Lehigh Valley morgue with Cap and Dave as Dr. Land performed the postmortem examination. He was rough with Xavier's body, and it bothered me.

The medical evidence was like a horror story in clinical terms.

Xavier had arrived at the Hazleton Hospital barely clinging to life. He had no spontaneous brain activity. His body temperature had dropped to 33.1 degrees Celsius—about 91.5 degrees Fahrenheit—so low, it meant his brain could no longer regulate body function.

He was limp. Lifeless. His pupils didn't respond to light. That's when it was obvious that this baby had suffered something devastating.

During the trial, Dr. Kerrie Pinkney, the pediatric intensivist, said she had immediately observed the signs of catastrophic trauma.

Calm and collected on the stand, she said, "He was critically ill. The fullness of the soft spot—his fontanelle—told me there was swelling in the brain. Bleeding. Trauma."

I found Dr. Pinkney to be compassionate and knowledgeable. She fought for Xavier and supported our team.

The CAT scan showed cerebral edema. The bleeding was extensive.

And there was bruising discovered and noted on the side of Xavier's foot. An imprint. "It's where someone likely gripped him," she said. And gripped hard.

Dr. Mark Trachtman, a pediatric ophthalmologist, also took the stand. He said he'd used a direct ophthalmoscope to examine Xavier's eyes. What he saw horrified him.

"A sea of red and black," he said in court. It was the worst retinal hemorrhaging he had ever seen. It wasn't just in one layer of the eye; it was in every layer. "That's from acceleration and deceleration," he told the jury. "That's shaking."

Shaken baby syndrome is one of the cruelest forms of abuse. The infant's brain, underdeveloped and fragile, slams against the inside of the skull. Capillaries burst.

Blood fills the space where life used to be. There's no mistaking it. No natural disease process mimics these injuries. No accident produces it so uniformly.

In Xavier's case, it was from rage. It was destruction. It was murder.

Dr. Land's autopsy and testimony revealed unspeakable brutality: skull fractures; contusions of the frontal scalp, right cheek, right inner lip, and left parieto-occipital scalp; a 4.5-centimeter horizontal fracture of the left posterior parietal bone; several severe subdural hematomas; subarachnoid hemorrhages; diffuse hemorrhage enveloping the spinal cord; suture separation of the bones of the skull; bilateral retinal hemorrhages; and extensive bruising to the legs and buttocks.

Injuries consistent with a whiplash-type action, along with contusion of the left thigh and the interior buttock, which is uncommon for a three-month-old.

Dr. Land paused in court and looked at the jury. "These are not injuries a three-month-old child sustains on his own. These are inflicted."

It dawned on me that Xavier was literally broken from head to toe.

There were audible gasps. Even after everything we'd presented, the words still landed like punches. This wasn't just a failure to protect. This was brutality.

And then, after inflicting these injuries, Alan Leitzel had lit a cigarette and left the room.

While Xavier's brain swelled and his eyes bled, Leitzel smoked a cigarette.

That image haunted me. And it will forever.

After the autopsy was completed and before we walked out, I approached Xavier's body. I touched Xavier's tiny hand. It barely filled my palm. I whispered, "I got you, little man."

That day changed me. We rode home for just over an hour. Dave and I had previously teased Cap mercilessly on our travels, but this time all I said was that it had been awful. We rode back from Allentown to Wilkes-Barre in uncharacteristic silence.

CHAPTER 9

THE TRIAL AND THE TRUTH THAT XAVIER DESERVED

WE PROSECUTED LEITZEL AGGRESSIVELY, AND his conviction for first-degree murder was swift. The judge sentenced Leitzel to life in prison without the possibility of parole. In most shaken-baby cases, the defendant is convicted of third-degree murder.

The incidents usually involve someone losing control when a child is crying. These cases are most often regarded as malicious killings and not first-degree or intentional murder with premeditation.

I believed in my heart that this case was different. I believed that Leitzel was not your typical defendant in a shaken-baby case, not by a long shot. I believed and wanted to prove that Leitzel had hated Xavier because he was Black. I used the racial epithets that he had used against Xavier to establish intent and motive to kill him. Leitzel had a swastika tattooed on his chest while awaiting trial. I argued that further showed who Leitzel was and that it was his intention to murder Xavier. In rebuttal, his defense attorney, Jonathan Blum, claimed that Alan suffered from a condition known as intermittent explosive disorder. I asked the defense expert, "Isn't this just another name for a bad temper?"

One of the aspects of this condition is that the "sufferer" regrets the actions he or she took during an episode.

I asked the doctor the defense brought in, "If you heard that Mr. Leitzel referred to baby Xavier after his death as an 'it' and an 'eggplant,' would you agree that doesn't sound like regret?"

The doctor agreed.

I used the fact that Leitzel had had a cigarette during his assault of Xavier and had walked downstairs at one point. I argued that these actions could and should have calmed him down. Yet he continued in his rage, which I argued constituted the intention to commit murder.

Under the law, the intent to commit murder can be formed in a fraction of a second. I said that Leitzel had had plenty of time to form the intent to kill Xavier, and his going downstairs and having a cigarette had all added to that level of intent.

But this was about more than just one monster. This was also about a mother who had failed spectacularly, a mother whose disregard for her child had led directly to his death.

Charging Tiffany with involuntary manslaughter drew skepticism. Some questioned pursuing her criminally, because she hadn't directly inflicted the fatal blows. But for our team and me, justice demanded accountability.

Tiffany had a sacred duty to protect Xavier, a legal and moral obligation etched clearly in black-and-white instructions in the safety plan. Her blatant disregard of repeated warnings and common sense had set the stage for her son's brutal murder. In my mind, her accountability was unquestionable.

I carried with me into that courtroom not just the evidence but the example set by my own mother and grandmother.

I thought of my grandmother, Ida, who had cleaned houses, gone without to feed my mother, and worn the same dress repeatedly, washing it each night by hand. I carried the warning from Nicole's grandmother, Mary, that no parent sleeps peacefully.

I thought of my mother, Rose, who had raised four boys alone and never failed in her duties, tirelessly working long hours for our future. She had climbed the corporate ladder with four boys clinging to her shoulders. Even when she was exhausted, we remained her priority.

What makes a mother? It's not biology. It's not instinct. It's love in action.

That was the standard that my mother and grandmother had set in my home. Their love was never passive. It was active, fierce, and given daily.

That's why Tiffany shattered something sacred in this case. She didn't just fail Xavier, she betrayed motherhood. A mother is the first defense, the final shield, the most sacred vow.

When that vow is broken, it echoes louder than even gunshots and stabbings. And that's why this case will follow me until I can no longer speak.

Tiffany had to be held accountable, not only to the law but to a standard of motherhood defined by women who knew sacrifice. Her guilt wasn't simply criminal; it was moral, ethical, and deeply personal.

In response to those letters Tiffany wrote to Leitzel, defense attorney Centini claimed they did nothing to advance our case, that they were an effort on my part to humiliate Tiffany. Centini asked why a prosecutor who thinks they have enough evidence to convict someone of a crime would resort to reading a love letter into the record if it proved no fact.

In one letter, as I mentioned earlier, Tiffany spoke lovingly of preparing Leitzel breakfast upon his release, calling him "baby."

I looked at the jury as I spoke, making sure the emotional weight wasn't lost. "She wrote thirteen pages and never once mentioned her dead son," I told them, emphasizing that she had written the letter five weeks after Xavier's death. "She knew it would upset Leitzel. That tells you all you need to know about Tiffany Simmons as a mother."

We even presented the testimony of a local news reporter, Andy Mehalsick of WBRE. Andy had been covering crime in Luzerne County for decades. When covering the death of Xavier Simmons, he had the opportunity to interview Tiffany. We called Andy for a bold move. He entered the courtroom imbued with decades of credibility. We played the video of her interview where she acted oblivious and ignorant of what happened to Xavier. This was a powerful piece of evidence and spoke volumes to our jury.

I remember every detail of the courtroom during that case. The creaks of the floors. The scent of old wood. The weight of the silence before the jury entered.

And most of all, the photo of Xavier Simmons—the one that a Children and Youth Services caseworker had taken just days before he was murdered. It showed him safe, smiling, in his grandmother's care.

In an effort to generate sympathy, the defense used a professional photograph of Tiffany holding Xavier. I objected to this photograph, arguing that it had no bearing on the case and would serve only to engender emotion in the jury. The judge allowed the framed portrait in, and I was not happy.

Centini then held the professionally framed photograph of Tiffany holding Xavier and showed it to the jury. She said, "Make no mistake, ladies and gentlemen, that she will never hold her precious son in her arms again. He was taken away from her forever. She will live the rest of her life not knowing how his second

Christmas would have been in a couple of weeks, not knowing what his first birthday would have been like, not feeling his first tooth as it popped through, not seeing him go off on his first day of school, not watching him play football, not watching him graduate from high school, go to his senior prom, and to give her grandchildren."

Finally, Centini said Tiffany was not at fault: "The Commonwealth's proof is not up here beyond a reasonable doubt. Come back here, come back here and tell her that she's not guilty, and don't be afraid to do it."

Centini summarized her defense of Tiffany in a compelling closing argument. She said Alan had never hit Xavier before, that Children and Youth Services hadn't felt that Xavier was in danger, or they would have taken him.

Despite all of the violence in Leitzel's past, she said, there had been no indication that he'd ever hurt a child. She argued that this was why Tiffany should not be convicted. She argued that Leitzel had killed Xavier in a rage, which also had not been foreseeable.

Centini's argument, coupled with her use of the picture and emotion, was strong. I had to respond in my closing.

My closing argument was as personal as it was prosecutorial. My mother would follow my cases in the press, and we would often discuss them. She would even come to court to watch parts of my trials. I would confer with her as I was working through a case. She would always provide some valuable insight. I asked her to attend the closing argument in Xavier's case, and she did. I needed her in my corner that day. She sat in the gallery beside Nicole.

It was December 12, 2008. I began by saying, "I'm going to tell you a story about a baby boy born to a single mother. He's biracial. He was born into a predominantly white community. He's going to be raised primarily by his maternal grandmother. He's going to have a lot of challenges. He's going to have to overcome them. What's going to become of this little biracial boy? Could he change the world? Could he overcome these challenges?"

I stopped for a moment of silence. The jurors stared at me, wondering what I was saying or where I was going.

I continued, "One month ago, that baby boy was elected president of the United States of America."

Of course, I was talking about Barack Obama. A man who, like Xavier, had come from complicated circumstances—raised by his grandmother, biracial, and often underestimated.

"Does that story sound familiar?" I continued. "Like the baby in the story, Xavier could have changed the world, but ladies and gentlemen, this isn't a story about what could have been. This is a case about what should have been."

You could have heard a pin drop.

Obama had just won. History was fresh in everyone's minds. Hope was fresh. The line "Xavier could have changed the world" wasn't just a rhetorical device. It was the truth. Xavier Simmons could have been anything. But now, he'd never be anything.

He had been reduced to a body in a bassinet, shipped to Lehigh Valley Hospital, and ultimately laid cold on a stainless-steel slab while I watched a doctor peel back the layers of what used to be life.

I said, "This case is about a mother who stood between her baby and a monster—and stepped aside."

I pointed to the love letter again. "Thirteen pages. Not one mention of Xavier."

I looked the jury in the eyes and told them what Xavier had endured. The suffocating internal pressure. The skull fracture. The blood pooling inside his tiny brain.

I repeated what Dr. Pinkney had said: "There was no blood flow to Xavier's brain. He was brain-dead." The jury winced, and I wanted them to. Because if this baby had to suffer, then we, too, had to feel that suffering to give it weight. To give it justice.

I raised my voice. I could feel the room tighten. "We are not here to talk about what Xavier could have been. We are here because of what he should have had: a mother."

I highlighted the red flags that Tiffany had recklessly ignored. Leitzel was violent. Leitzel was ill-tempered. Leitzel had cost her the custody of her three other children.

Most of all, Leitzel had harbored racial hate toward Xavier. Tiffany had never told Children and Youth Services the truth about that fact. She'd ignored the safety plan. She'd failed to wake up and protect Xavier. All of these factors together constituted a recklessness that led to Xavier's death and, I argued, constituted involuntary manslaughter.

I carefully reviewed our testimony. I revisited the testimony so it was fresh in their minds.

I ended by walking over to that professional photo. I stared at the picture of Tiffany holding Xavier. I was silent. And I let the silence land. Centini had left the photo propped on the defense table near Tiffany and facing the jury. I picked it up.

I said, "They are trying to protect her with the image of this baby."

I yelled, "How dare she? He was a gift, and she squandered him. She failed to protect him." I took the photo and placed it on my table, and said, "She doesn't deserve him. He's with us."

Even as I write this now, I can feel the hush in that room. As if we had all stopped breathing.

Justice would come, but it would never be enough for Xavier.

As I paced in front of the jury, part of me was still standing at the side of my son's crib in the dead of night, watching him breathe. I could see my wife, Nicole, who is an incredible mother, caring for my son, too.

There is a line, invisible but real, that separates the prosecutor from the father in me. I felt it in my partner, Dave Pedri, a young father who fought this case with me. But during this trial, that line became blurred. We crossed it. We weren't just litigating the murder of Xavier; We were mourning him. Mourning him as a father might. I thought about the late nights with my own newborn. The sleeplessness. The exhaustion. The overwhelming love.

Tiffany chose sleep over protection. That haunted me and still does today.

I had to reckon with the part of myself that knew how precious a few hours of rest are for a new parent, and the part of me that knew she had no excuse. I've never been the same since.

This wasn't about whether Tiffany was grieving. It was about whether she acted with reckless disregard for her son's life. She had choices. She made them. And Xavier is dead because of them.

I choked up and raised my voice as I spoke my final words to the jury: "It's too late to save him, it's too late to protect him, but it's not too late for justice."

On December 12, 2008, the jury was sent out to deliberate at 5:45 p.m., and at 7:35 p.m., they announced that they had reached a verdict. We were herded back into the courtroom. I sat at the prosecution table with Dave and Cap. The judge asked the foreperson to read the verdict. Tiffany Simmons was found guilty of involuntary manslaughter and of endangering the welfare of a child, and the jurors had found an enhancement that Tiffany engaged in a reckless course of conduct, not simply one act. She was then sentenced to twenty-five to fifty months in state prison.

A sentence short of the permanency of her actions upon Xavier's life, but a lawful sentence for involuntary manslaughter.

I left the courthouse and later went to a holiday dinner with Nicole and my law partners at Bill Finnegan's home. The home was filled with children and the people I learned to trust. Cases and moments like this break your heart but make you appreciate the good people in your life.

CHAPTER 10

THE LEGACY OF XAVIER SIMMONS

AFTER THE TRIAL, WHEN THE foreperson read the verdict, I didn't feel triumphant. I felt exhausted, relieved, and the lingering ache of injustice.

We convicted both Alan Leitzel and Tiffany Simmons. Xavier's killers were behind bars. But no sentence could bring that child back.

And no conviction could erase what I'd seen in that autopsy room.

I kept the picture of Xavier that the caseworker had taken days before his death. In it, he's smiling and sleeping peacefully, dressed in a little blue onesie. He had no idea what was coming. That image sits in my office to this day, seventeen years later. It reminds me that no matter what I have going on, I was given the honor of fighting for that little baby.

I've prosecuted cases in which the victims were adults—men and women with stories, jobs, friends, and flaws. But Xavier was different. He had no voice. No mistakes. No second chances. Just a tiny baby in a blue onesie.

When I spoke of him in court, I was not just recounting facts; I was resurrecting him. I wanted the jury to hear his cries, to imagine his laughter, to know what we'd lost.

I know that being in that room and seeing Xavier's autopsy tore me apart and permanently damaged me. Many prosecutors and I endure secondary trauma from occurrences such as this.

But I have to believe it was worth it.

There's a quote I love, used by novelist Dennis Lehane but originally attributed to writer Eleanor Brownn: "You cannot serve from an empty vessel." But cases like this emptied me. I gave everything I had, because Xavier had nothing left. And sometimes, I wonder if that's why I keep his picture so close. To refill me.

Xavier Simmons will never become president. But in our courtroom, for one shining moment, he became a symbol of justice, and a voice too powerful to ignore.

We remember him not just for what he lost, but for what he taught us to protect. That's the legacy I carry.

This case didn't make national news. It wasn't the kind of story that carried headlines for months. But it carried weight. It mattered. And it fits the theme of this book in every way. Not every mother is a hero. Some fail. Some fail so catastrophically that it becomes our duty—as prosecutors, as human beings—to hold them accountable.

When Tiffany walked into that courtroom, she thought she was being judged by the law. But she was also being measured against women like my mother and grandmother. And she came up short.

That's what drove me. That's what kept me up at night reading her letters, combing through records, building this case. I wasn't just prosecuting a negligent mother. In my heart, I was standing up for every mother who had ever fought for their child, who had protected them at all costs.

I often get asked: "Can you forgive someone like Tiffany Simmons?" And the honest answer is, I don't know. There's a part of me, the father part, that sees only red. That wants to damn her for eternity.

But there's another part, a quieter part, that sees her own upbringing, her ignorance, her desperation. It doesn't excuse what she did, but it explains some of it. The world is complicated.

My duty wasn't to pity her; it was to prosecute her.

My job wasn't to forgive—it was to hold criminals accountable. But I do know this: we're at our most human when we allow room for both accountability and complexity. That's what this case taught me.

I wish I could say Xavier was the first and only baby murder that I handled, but there were many more to come. In the prosecution, your reward for success is tougher and more cases.

I eventually prosecuted two separate mothers who abused their babies, both of whom survived for years in a comatose state before death.

I prosecuted a mother who left her little girl in a room for twenty-eight hours and she dehydrated and died.

I prosecuted a mother whose child died when she exposed her to packets of fentanyl.

I am haunted by a little girl who survived horrific abuse, as I can still see an injury to her face that looked like a piece was missing. She had bilateral burns on her arms from a rope that held her to a plastic little bed.

All of them were prosecuted and held accountable but it began with little Xavier.

I had a mother who put me and my brothers ahead of everything. I owed it to her to prosecute mothers who failed to do the same. My mother told me to help a mother in need, but she also set a standard that others were measured against.

CHAPTER 11

THE BOY WHO WATCHES OVER ME

FOUR YEARS LATER: JANUARY 29, 2013. I was in New Orleans, Louisiana, during Super Bowl week, attending Media Day at the then Mercedes-Benz Superdome. The streets contained sets for CBS television shows that were broadcasting live.

As the event was letting out, I was walking through Jackson Square, swallowed by a sea of humanity. The streets were packed with television crews, vendors, and thousands of excited football fans. Local vendors lined the path. Many of them were unmistakably from New Orleans, adorned in the proud traditions of the Big Easy—bright colors, layered textures, and expressions that told their own stories.

Out of the corner of my eye, I noticed a fortune teller sitting at a small table beneath a faded sign that read "The Voo Doo Bone Lady." She wore a regal shawl, her clothing vibrant and theatrical, perfectly suited for the city's mysticism.

I turned to my brother-in-law, Dr. Christopher Sanders—a world-class plastic surgeon, a devoted sci-fi nerd, and one of my closest friends—and said, "Let's go see the fortune teller. Let's see what she has to say."

Nothing about us screamed professionalism or prosecutor that day. I was in a long-sleeved T-shirt and cargo shorts, relaxed and unsuspecting. I sat down across from her, and she began to read my fortune. Without hesitation, she looked at me and said she saw a child around me. He had dark hair and dark eyes—a child who, she said, was my guardian. "He has no name," she told me. "Or maybe just an X for his name." She asked if my wife and I had ever lost a child.

"No," I replied. "We've never lost a child."

She paused, then continued. "This child...he looks like you. He's dark-complected, with dark eyes and dark hair. He's protecting you."

I was stunned. I told her that there *was* a child in my life who fit that description. A boy named Xavier, sometimes referred to as "Baby X" by Tiffany and Alan, the people who had failed him. And I told her the truth. He had been born. He had died tragically. And I had prosecuted the people responsible for his death.

She nodded confidently, her voice steady. "He watches you now."

That exchange has never left me. It rattled me then. It still shakes me now.

To this day, in moments of doubt or need, I find myself thinking of Xavier. Sometimes I even ask for his help. I don't know if he's truly there, but it helps to believe he is.

And maybe that's enough.

I couldn't believe what I was hearing that day in Jackson Square, but I was grateful to hear it. As I continued my prosecutions—each case heavy, each one personal—I often glanced at that picture of Xavier, that beautiful little boy who could have been anything.

Maybe even president.

LESSONS IN MOTIVATION: WHAT WE FIGHT FOR

Here, we confront the rawest edge of justice: where law meets love, and where failure is not theoretical but fatal.

Xavier Simmons never had a chance to tell his story, so I did it for him. Through the grief, anger, and resolve I felt for him, we're reminded that motivation doesn't always spring from triumph. Sometimes it is born from heartbreak.

We don't always choose the cases or the moments that shape us. But we do choose how we respond.

We can choose to act when others retreat. We can choose accountability over excuses. And we can choose to carry the stories of the voiceless, even when they're too heavy for words.

The courtroom isn't just a battleground for law. It's a place where memory, sacrifice, and legacy intersect. Xavier's case shows us what happens when systems fail, when love turns into betrayal, and when justice must pick up the pieces.

Motivation, here, is not about ambition. It's about honoring the sacred vow to protect the vulnerable, especially when they have no one else.

Let that be your reminder: the most powerful fuel comes not from what we gain, but from what we refuse to lose.

ACCOUNTABILITY AS A COMPASS FOR PURPOSE

Not every story ends with healing.

Not every courtroom offers closure wrapped in grace.

In the case of Xavier Simmons, what remained was not forgiveness but a demand for accountability, an unrelenting pursuit of responsibility in the face of senseless harm.

Accountability isn't just a legal principle; it's a moral one. From the story of Xavier, we see that when systems falter, when parents fail, and when evil finds its way into the cradle of a child, someone must stand up and hold the line. Someone must name what happened and demand consequences.

My motivation didn't come from a higher sense of peace or moral absolution. It came from duty. It came from standing over the lifeless body of a three-month-old boy and knowing that silence would be complicity. It came from watching a mother choose her abuser over her son, and recognizing that justice, at its core, is about drawing hard lines in the sand—lines that protect the vulnerable and confront those who harm.

What can we ultimately learn from this?

Accountability begins with recognition. We cannot fix what we're unwilling to face. And in our lives, whether we're prosecutors, parents, leaders, or simply people trying to do the right thing, we must face the discomfort of truth. We must recognize when harm has occurred, and we must be willing to do the hard, often thankless work of responding to it with clarity and conviction.

Accountability is not revenge. It is not about punishment for the sake of punishment. It is about responsibility. It is about standing before the world and saying, *This happened. This mattered. And we will not look away.*

It's also a mirror. In confronting Tiffany Simmons and Alan Leitzel and the mothers that followed, I also had to confront the broader systems that had enabled them—systems of social services, of generational trauma, of race and poverty, and of apathy. And in doing so, I revealed a deeper motivation: not just to prosecute a case but to prevent future ones.

So, how do we embrace this kind of motivation in our own lives?

We take responsibility, even when it's easier to deflect. We ask hard questions. We challenge the silence. And, most important, we refuse to allow pain, especially the pain of the innocent, to be erased without consequence.

Because justice isn't about how things should be. It's about ensuring that even when the world fails a child like Xavier Simmons, someone will still show up and say, *No more.*

Let that be your guide. In a world full of injustice, your motivation might not always be soft. Sometimes it must be fierce. Sometimes your purpose is to stand in the rubble and be the one who says, *This stops here.*

Book 4

THE MOVIE STAR MURDERER

Commonwealth v. Hugo Selenski

"It had struck me that the world was full of holes, holes which you could fall into, never to be seen again. I couldn't understand the difference between disappearance and death. Both seemed the same to me, both left holes. Holes in your heart holes in your life."

—Sally Gardner, *Maggot Moon*

CHAPTER 1

GONE

SOMETIMES EVIL DOESN'T KICK THE door in. It slips in through the cracks. Smiles at you. Sits at your table. Says, "Trust me."

May 3, 2002. The last normal day that Gerry and Michael Kerkowski Sr. ("Senior") would ever know.

Gerry was doing what many mothers do when the world around them starts to fall apart—she was trying to hold it all together.

She and Senior, her husband, a retired banker, had built a quiet life in Northeastern Pennsylvania. They had raised two boys and watched them grow into men and become fathers themselves, and now Gerry and Senior were grandparents.

But the family was unraveling.

Their son, Michael Jr., was in trouble. For the past year and a half, he had been locked in a bitter custody-and-divorce battle, while also facing serious charges for the illegal sale of prescription painkillers from the small pharmacy in Tunkhannock that he owned.

His license. His livelihood. His boys. His freedom. All of it was at risk.

Senior had been managing the mounting legal and financial stresses while Gerry worked the counter at her son's pharmacy.

But the tension in the house, in the family, had become constant. On May 1, 2002, two days before everything changed, the Kerkowskis had dinner at Michael's home.

As Gerry would later remember, they cleaned up together afterward, and Gerry helped bathe her grandsons, Tyler and Connor. Michael stood in the kitchen as she gathered her things to leave.

"Thank you for everything, Mom. I love you," he said.

It would be the last time she ever heard her son's voice.

Two days later, Gerry called Michael's house around 2:30 p.m. Tammy Fassett—Michael's girlfriend—answered. Tammy had been a rare light in Michael's increasingly dark world.

She worked at the bagel shop beside his pharmacy. Like Michael, she had gone through a hard divorce. They'd found each other when both were broken, and together they'd built something that looked like healing.

Gerry invited them over to see the new television she and Senior had bought. Tammy said they might stop by before or after Michael picked up his sons from daycare at 4:30 p.m.

Then, before hanging up, Tammy added, "We have company." She didn't sound concerned, but she didn't say who the company was.

Gerry didn't press.

By 4:30 p.m., the lot outside Little People daycare in Kingston had become crowded with parents picking up their children on what had become a beautiful spring day. Within minutes, the lot emptied.

But two small boys, Tyler, age five, and Connor, age three, remained. Michael, their father, hadn't come. He had dropped them off that morning. It was his day to pick them up. And Michael was never late. Never.

The teacher checked the time. It was 4:45 p.m. No sign of Michael. She called his house. No answer. She called the boys' mother, Kim Kerkowski. No answer. She called the grandparents, Senior and Gerry. Nothing. She called their aunt. Still no answer.

By 5 p.m., her unease turned into dread. Something was wrong.

Michael and Tammy never came by to see the new television. The Kerkowskis assumed that something had come up. But even as they had dinner at the Central Hotel in Sullivan County and did some shopping, the unease lingered. They arrived home around 10 p.m.

That's when Gerry checked the answering machine.

The first message was from the daycare. Michael hadn't picked up the boys. The second was from Kim, and it was scathing. She screamed into the machine, demanding to know where Michael was, furious that he hadn't picked up his sons. She ended the message with a bitter curse: "I hope he's dead in a ditch somewhere."

Her words hung heavy in the room.

Kim, at least, had picked up the boys by then. But Michael's unexplained absence—it wasn't like him. Panic began to build.

Gerry and Senior called Michael's home. No answer.

They drove out to Hunlock Creek, where Michael lived. The house sat quiet atop a hill on a country road, nestled into manicured landscaping. Michael was proud of his home. But things felt wrong the moment the Kerkowskis pulled into the driveway.

Michael's Ford F-150 was parked head-in, not backed in as usual. Tammy's 1991 Dodge sedan was also there. The John Deere tractor in the garage was facing the wrong way. A chair was holding the screen door into the house from the garage open.

Inside, more strange signs.

Michael's security monitor, normally always on, was off. The VHS tapes used to record surveillance were gone. The camera, usually trained on the driveway, had been tilted up to the ceiling.

The wooden rolling pin that normally hung on the kitchen wall was missing.

The Kerkowskis climbed the stairs. Michael's wallet was on his nightstand, and his credit cards and cash were untouched. Tammy's tennis bracelet and ring were beside her overnight bag, still on the bed. Nothing was packed. Nothing appeared missing.

In the guest room, the mostly pink bedspread was gone, as was a new bedspread that had still been in its packaging they had seen prior.

Everything else was in place. The doors were locked, the windows shut, the carpets had fresh vacuum lines, and the vacuum cleaner was sitting out.

Downstairs in the finished basement, Senior found the rolling pin. It had been shoved under the couch. One of the handles was bent. There were marks on it.

Michael rarely left town. And when he did, he told his parents. But now, no note, no call, and no signs of departure. Tammy was gone. Michael was gone.

They started making calls. Gerry reached Tammy's sister, Lisa Sands. She hadn't heard from Tammy, and said Tammy hadn't come home. Lisa was concerned but not alarmed at that point. Tammy and Lisa were not only sisters but best friends. They told each other everything.

The Kerkowskis debated calling the police. But Michael's ongoing legal battles had soured their relationship with law enforcement.

They didn't know who to trust.

But they did know who Michael trusted.

They called a man Michael had once described as the only one he trusted more than his attorneys: his best friend, Hugo Selenski.

CHAPTER 2

THE BIRTH AND THE FRIEND

ON AUGUST 1, 1973, AT 12:14 p.m., in Sioux City, Iowa, Hugo Marcus Friend was born at St. Joseph's Mercy Hospital to Robert and Ruth Ann Friend.

Robert had come from a prominent family in the Midwest. His family owned a large commercial building in downtown Sioux City.

In time, Robert and Ruth Ann would have two daughters as well—Ruth Ann and Mary Ann. The marriage lasted just five years before ending in divorce.

Robert Friend had a reputation. Devilishly handsome. Charismatic. But always scheming.

In 1983, he was working as a gem salesman when he disappeared with more than a million dollars' worth of jewels—gems he was supposed to be showing on behalf of his employer, not stashing away in a bank under his own name. The authorities were called. Charges were filed. A warrant was issued.

He vanished.

For nine months, Robert Friend was on the run, rumored to have fled the country. But he slipped up. He tried crossing the Mexican border in El Paso, Texas, under his real name, a mistake he'd later call "a blooper."

In 1984, wearing a navy-blue suit and cowboy boots, Robert resurfaced in Luzerne County court. Still arrogant and elusive, he refused to say what had happened to the missing jewels.

He pleaded guilty to theft charges and served two years in county prison, paying $125,000 in restitution. Most of the gems were never recovered. After prison, Robert moved to Las Vegas and had little to no contact with his children.

Ruth Ann, his ex-wife, on the other hand, was a local girl. She was from Pittston, Pennsylvania, and was a beautiful woman by every account. Many who knew her said she had been the prettiest girl in school. And just as quickly, they'd mention her fondness for and struggles with alcohol.

In 1979, she returned to Northeastern Pennsylvania and married a bank examiner named Ronald Selenski. They settled in Dallas, Pennsylvania, an area known as the Back Mountain. Ronald adopted her children, and Hugo Friend became Hugo Selenski.

The couple raised Hugo in the suburbs, alongside his two sisters. Ruth Ann and Ronald would go on to have four more children together.

As a boy, Hugo showed promise in sports. He was fast, naturally athletic, a standout in Little League and youth football. He attended Catholic elementary school before switching to public schools for junior and senior high.

He played quarterback in junior high but was eventually kicked off the team for skipping practices. His behavior was growing more erratic and antisocial.

By high school, Hugo was abusing alcohol and collecting criminal charges: burglary, receiving stolen property, criminal conspiracy, motorcycle thefts, and driving under the influence and with a suspended license.

His mother, Ruth Ann, reported to juvenile authorities that he had "an occasional violent temper" and would become "very physical."

By 1991, he had fathered a daughter with a classmate. At the end of high school, a report card listed him as ranking 150 out of 151 students. His classmates voted him Most Likely to Be in Detention.

A juvenile court evaluation described him as being immature and lazy. He needed structure, adult guidance, and alcohol counseling. But he violated probation, skipped meetings with his officers, and continued spiraling.

After high school, Hugo was planning to join the Marine Corps. But before he could enlist, he crashed a motorcycle and sustained serious injuries.

Once he recovered, he joined the Marines and was shipped off to basic training at Parris Island in South Carolina. Those who saw him after boot camp noticed a shift. He was more polite. More respectful.

But that didn't last.

He was kicked out of the Marines after it was discovered that he had failed to disclose a three-thousand-dollar debt owed to Luzerne County juvenile court.

Out of the service, Hugo drifted from job to job—warehouse work, a plastics factory, restaurants, and a laundry. He rarely had steady work. He picked up more DUI charges and served time.

In January 1994, he had a second daughter with a girlfriend named Carey Bartoo. Later, he fathered a third child with another woman.

By the summer of 1994, Hugo's life was falling apart. His criminal behavior had grown darker. He was no longer just careless; he was reckless and dangerous.

On June 10, 1994, Hugo and an accomplice named Earl Naugle robbed the Mellon Bank in Plains Township. They wore ski masks and carried semiautomatic weapons.

Hugo entered the bank and aimed his gun at the manager. She kept her hands firmly on the desk and was unable to trip the silent alarm.

Another teller moved just slightly, and her leg bumped a drawer.

Hugo turned the gun on her, racked it, and said not to move again. The teller would later say she had been overwhelmed by one thought: she had never had children and would never become a mother. She thought she was going to die. She handed over the money.

In a car they had stolen, Hugo and Naugle fled with a bag containing cash, but it was packed with dye and gas explosives. Once outside the bank's sensors, the dye packs exploded, staining the cash and filling the air with red smoke.

The gas caused burning in their eyes and lungs. Witnesses reported seeing the getaway car trailing smoke, the windows open, and the two men waving the ruined money outside in frustration.

Hugo skipped town to Las Vegas, to his father's home, just ahead of the authorities' arrival at the home of Ruth Ann and Ronald. But the feds were close behind. Days later, federal agents raided two homes owned by Ruth Ann and Ronald Selenski. They found four thousand dollars in cash, along with ammo and clothing soaked in red dye.

Hugo had tried to run the bills through a washing machine in a failed attempt to "launder" the evidence.

He was indicted and eventually returned to Pennsylvania to surrender.

At nineteen, while his classmates were heading to college or beginning careers, Hugo Selenski pled guilty to bank robbery charges and was sentenced to seven years in the Federal Correctional Institution Lewisburg, a medium-security prison.

There, he met a man named Paul Weakley.

Paul had a different story, but he was cut from the same cloth. Born in Michigan, he grew up normal until his father died young of multiple sclerosis.

When his father died, Paul broke. Petty crime turned into full-blown felonies. He built bombs. Stole military vans. Lived in ice cream shops and abandoned dorm rooms.

He was smart—memorized electronics manuals and studied everything he could while locked up. Intelligence can make men like Paul even more dangerous.

Hugo and Paul built a small criminal syndicate inside the walls of Lewisburg.

Marijuana deals. Postage stamps used as currency. At some point, Hugo owed Paul seventeen thousand dollars. Hugo promised to pay it back when they got out.

And Hugo said that when Paul got out, he'd have a place for him. A plan. A new life.

But it wasn't about a new life. It was about a new hustle.

On January 19, 2001, Hugo was released from FCI Lewisburg. He was narcissistic, violent, fearless, and reckless. He was incapable of living a normal life, the same scenario that plays out with some people when they return from tours in the military. Many simply can't adapt. They struggle. And the same was true for Hugo.

All that remained of him was a better criminal. And he was building a criminal kingdom in the Pennsylvania woods.

Michael Kerkowski was going to be his first crown jewel.

CHAPTER 3

HOME

HUGO WAS LIVING IN THE basement of his adoptive father's house, under the watchful, tired eye of Ronald Selenski Sr.

Hugo wasn't doing well.

Prison had changed him, but not in the ways people hoped for. He couldn't stand crowds. His anxiety was suffocating in public. He had child support bills piling up and was still under the terms of parole.

An uncle gave him work with a construction crew, and on the surface, Hugo looked like he was trying. It looked like he was rebuilding. But those who looked closer saw the cracks widening.

That fall, just after the 9/11 attacks paralyzed the nation, Hugo reconnected with Christina Strom, a woman he'd known previously through mutual friends.

Tina was in her twenties; sharp, attractive, and ambitious. She worked in insurance by day, bartended by night, and lived in a small house on Miller Street in Luzerne that her grandmother had left her. Tina was in a good place, or so she thought.

And then Hugo entered her life.

They ran into each other at a bar. Reconnection turned to flirtation, and within weeks, Hugo was living with her. Tina's brother, who had been sharing the home, quietly moved out. Tina later wouldn't even remember asking Hugo to move in.

That was his method: ease in, charm, manipulate, occupy. Her friends tried to warn her. He had a past. He had a record. But Tina, both nurturing and naive, believed she could fix him. Hugo disarmed women using his bad-boy image, good looks, and charm.

She couldn't fix him.

Carey Bartoo, the former girlfriend of Hugo, who was the mother of his second daughter, knew better. Carey and Hugo had a toxic history. She had struggled somewhat with drug use in the past, but after an injury she was prescribed opioids—and like so many in those circumstances, she fell hard into addiction.

By the time Hugo returned from prison, Carey had become a shell of herself, gripped tightly by heroin. Carey, like just about everyone in this circle, was beautiful but struggling. Their daughter was living with Carey's parents. Hugo and Carey had a friendly and often contentious relationship during this time.

Carey, now desperate and broke, would often hit up her cousin, Kim Kerkowski, for cash. Kim, once a well-to-do wife living in a big house with Michael Kerkowski, was now living in government housing in Back Mountain.

Her divorce from Michael had metaphorically burned everything down. Carey and Kim found themselves neighbors in defeat, broken by different means but equally disillusioned.

One day Carey asked Michael if she could borrow a few hundred dollars. She needed a ride to pick up the money at his house in Hunlock Creek and she asked Hugo to take her.

Hugo drove Carey out to Michael's, and she introduced him to Michael. Hugo shook Michael's hand, smiled, and saw exactly what Michael was—an opportunity.

Michael Kerkowski was also a man spiraling. Once a respected pharmacist, he had been arrested for illegally distributing OxyContin, accused of running a pill mill from his pharmacy. Michael's pharmacy was speculated to be one of the largest distributors of painkillers in the state. Michael's case had garnered some media attention, including reports of the large amounts of money involved in his operation.

The case had made headlines. His marriage was over. He had been indicted, tried, convicted, and was looking at serious prison time.

Hugo played it cool.

He talked like a guy who knew things. Claimed he'd learned how to navigate the system while locked up. Claimed he could help. Claimed he was different now. Michael, desperate and panicking, listened. And Hugo, with the instincts of a predator, leaned in.

Soon, Hugo was helping or claiming to help Michael review court filings, talking strategy, pretending to be a legal mind.

He convinced Michael that he could help him beat or reduce the charges. Michael was nerdy, heavyset, and insecure, and was drawn to Hugo's confidence, his athleticism, his edge. Hugo began showing up more.

Eventually, Michael told his parents, Senior and Gerry, "This is my friend Hugo. I trust him more than my lawyers." He told them that Hugo was his "best friend," and meant it.

Hugo started visiting the home of Gerry and Senior, too. He talked law. Talked strategy. He made an impression on Gerry.

She believed he was trying to help. Hugo visited on an occasion and was having coffee with the Kerkowskis. She would later remember asking why he shaved his head and was covered in tattoos. "To look tough," he said.

Gerry was happy that Michael had someone like Hugo on his side. She thought Hugo gave Michael a fighting chance.

But behind the charm was the con.

At one point, Michael asked Senior to hide sixty thousand dollars in cash—money he didn't want Kim to know about. Senior agreed. Together, they stashed it inside a duct behind insulation in a wall. Just the two of them knew.

By early 2002, Hugo had become fully embedded in Michael's world.

Michael's trial came. Hugo was supposed to tamper with jurors, disrupt things, tip the scales. But he didn't do any of that. Instead, he sat in the gallery of the old Wyoming County Courthouse and glared at the judge.

Judge Brendan Vanston remembered those eyes—cold, flat, watching. Judge Vanston had seen countless criminals throughout his years on the bench, but he would later note that he'd never forget Hugo's cold eyes glaring at him.

Michael was convicted of dealing drugs and unlawfully dispensing prescriptions from his pharmacy.

He was now a felon, awaiting sentencing. Hugo's claimed manipulation of the system hadn't worked, but the relationship had already run deep.

Hugo knew about the money Michael had made. Knew about the house. Knew about the family. And now, the man who had once stood in the Kerkowskis' kitchen sipping coffee, the man Gerry had welcomed and tried to understand, was thinking about what came next.

And it wasn't about helping Michael.

It was about taking everything he could and picking the bones before the door slammed shut.

CHAPTER 4

MICHAEL KERKOWSKI PAYS FOR HIS OWN GRAVE

PAUL WEAKLEY WALKED OUT OF FCI Lewisburg in March 2002, quiet and lean. Tina Strom and her friend Ellen Smaka greeted him at the gate. Hugo could not pick Paul up because they technically weren't allowed to associate, based on the conditions of their parole. The three drove to a nearby McDonald's, where Hugo was waiting.

Hugo and Paul embraced like old friends, bonded by shared years behind bars and things they'd never speak of outside prison walls.

Tina, feeling charitable and a little sorry for Paul, let him move into the small Miller Street home she shared with Hugo. She helped Paul find work repairing water filters, helped him open a bank account—simple things that made her feel like she was doing something good.

Hugo had secured a friend's address that Paul would misrepresent as his address, due to parole's prohibiting their living together.

Tina had no idea she was now living with two killers.

Around that time, Hugo began obsessing over a house and its land in Back Mountain, a property tucked away on Mount

Olivet Road. It was private. Remote. Quiet. The house was located on a hill, on a wooded 6.1-acre property—just the kind of place Hugo needed.

The property belonged to an old-timer named Robert Steiner, an aging man with his own history of run-ins with the law and a collection of decaying Corvettes. Locals called him "Corvette Bob." Hugo had known him when he was a child and knew now that he was planning to move to Florida.

Hugo brought Tina up to see the place. She liked it well enough, but they both acknowledged that it needed a lot of work. Hugo assured Tina that he and his friends would rehab the property.

Paul liked it, too.

Not long after, Paul noticed what Hugo was really doing—stringing along Michael Kerkowski, manipulating him, preying on his fear. He asked Hugo, "What's the deal with this guy?"

Hugo didn't flinch. He told Paul plainly: Michael had millions in hidden cash, and the plan was to rob him. And if needed, kill him.

At first, Paul wanted no part of it. He told Hugo it was a terrible idea. Michael's case was too public, too volatile. Michael, meanwhile, had just paid Hugo between sixty thousand and eighty thousand dollars, supposedly for "legal services."

He and Paul tossed the cash onto a bed and counted it like schoolboys. Hugo used some of the money to pay debts, including what he owed Paul, and to pay bills.

The rest of the cash vanished fast. Hugo used thirty-two thousand dollars of it as an off-the-books cash down payment to Corvette Bob for the property. He spent another ten thousand dollars buying his younger brother, Ronnie, a car. Another twelve thousand dollars paid off Tina's credit cards. He gave Paul money for an apartment; Paul leased a place in Kingston and prepaid a year's rent. Hugo handed Paul more money to buy a green Dodge Avenger.

By April 30, 2002, the house on Mount Olivet Road had been officially purchased—at least on paper. The purchase price of the home was $160,000. Tina Strom was the listed buyer and secured a mortgage.

She'd written a down payment check for just over ten thousand dollars, but the bank account behind her check had just seven hundred dollars in it. Tina was panicking because the check would have to clear in the coming days and she didn't have the funds. Hugo had promised to handle it, promised that more money would come.

Corvette Bob was going to remain on the property for two additional weeks while he prepared to move to Florida. Hugo and Tina would move in after.

Tina pressed Hugo about the check in the days that followed, and Paul watched it all unravel. Finally, Hugo told her he'd get the money from Michael. Tina had no idea how Hugo was planning on securing the money.

Michael's sentencing was looming. The clock was ticking. Tina's check would bounce and undo the house closing. The window to act was closing.

Paul witnessed how panicked Tina was over the check. Hugo again approached him about robbing Michael. Hugo said they could make it look like Michael had fled due to his pending incarceration. Paul agreed to help, as he felt authorities would think that Michael had fled. They made the decision to rob—and, if necessary, kill—Michael Kerkowski. On May 2, 2002, they gathered duct tape, industrial flex ties, and wire cutters.

On May 3, 2002, Paul tucked the items into his cargo pants. He pre-looped flex ties and tucked them near the small of his back. He brought wire cutters and gloves, too. Hugo carried a gun and hid it under his shirt. They left for Michael's house.

Upon arrival at Michael's, they pulled up the long driveway in Hunlock Creek. Michael was cutting the grass on his John Deere tractor, and Tammy was whacking weeds nearby. Paul had thought it would just be Michael, but Tammy was there, too. He said Tammy was a "curveball."

Surprised but not shaken, and without hesitation while pulling into the driveway, Hugo and Paul decided right there that "she had to go"—meaning they'd kill Tammy, too. It would be cleaner that way. Tammy was wearing safety glasses. Hugo joked and said, "I wonder if she has a bulletproof vest."

Hugo and Paul got out of the car, and Michael approached them. Their visit was unexpected, but Michael invited them inside. They all went into the house. Paul described it later as an awkward visit.

Beers were passed around. The four of them made small talk. Michael mentioned that he had to pick up his sons from daycare. Paul looked at Hugo. Time was running out. Michael was expected somewhere.

Sometime between 2:30 and 4:30 p.m., Hugo pulled a gun and ordered Michael and Tammy to "get the fuck on the floor." Michael at first thought they were joking.

Hugo and Paul tied the couple up, putting flex ties around Tammy's wrists and ankles. She cried, "Why are you doing this?" They led Michael down to the basement at gunpoint while Tammy remained bound on the kitchen floor. They sat Michael on a small footstool.

Paul returned to the kitchen, carried Tammy upstairs, and told her to be quiet. "This isn't about you," he said. But that was a lie.

Paul headed back downstairs and, on his way down, grabbed a wooden rolling pin from the kitchen wall. He would say later that he saw it as a "tool of interrogation."

In the basement, Hugo and Paul bound Michael tighter. They wrapped duct tape around his face and eyes, his chest, his legs. Paul made ten passes with the duct tape around Michael's hands and wrists, which were already bound with a flex tie.

They beat him with the wooden rolling pin. Paul would say later that he beat Michael with the rolling pin "to inflict pain and enhance the fear factor." They cinched flex ties around his neck, tightening them until he gave up the location of a twenty-thousand-dollar stash in the ceiling.

Still not satisfied, they tortured him until he gave up another forty thousand dollars. They were pushing for the combination to Michael's safe. Michael told them it required two keys and Senior had one. Desperate, Michael said there was more money at his father's house. He begged them to just let them go and he would get it for them.

They didn't.

They kept tightening ties. Cutting one off, applying another. Renowned forensic pathologist Dr. Michael Baden would later testify that Michael's Adam's apple and hyoid bone were fractured, and that the amount and direction of the marks indicated that multiple ligatures had been utilized in the strangulation and torture. He would testify that the flex tie had been against Michael's spine. He would further note that Michael's body had signs of trauma consistent with being beaten with the rolling pin on his forehead, his knee, and the side of his head.

Dr. Baden would also testify that the duct tape around Michael's hands measured ten feet in length.

Michael may have gone into shock. At some point, he couldn't speak anymore. Hugo and Paul pulled the last tie tighter around Michael's neck, the one that killed him. Dr. Baden would later say it was so tight, a finger couldn't have slid under it.

Then Hugo went upstairs.

Tammy was still tied. Hugo used a flex tie to strangle her, too.

Tight. Effective. Silent.

Dr. Baden would later call the flex tie the perfect strangulation tool, as it wrapped the entire neck, cutting off air from every angle. Tammy died quickly.

Hugo and Paul dragged the bodies into the kitchen. Wrapped them in blankets and comforters. Paul propped open the screen door into the garage. They moved Michael's car out and pulled Paul's green Avenger into the garage.

They loaded the bodies into Paul's car, then pulled the car out and drove Michael's vehicle back into the garage, along with the tractor. Hugo stayed behind to clean up. Paul drove off with the dead.

A neighbor later saw Hugo being picked up by someone in a brown four-door car.

The next day, May 4, Hugo walked into the UFCW credit union with nearly $9,900 in cash, mostly twenties and fifties. Bank teller Cheryl Breen would later recall this strange encounter and that Hugo had told her he was buying a house for his girlfriend. She would say that she would never forget his eyes.

On Sunday, May 5, the bodies were still in Paul's car. Tammy in the back seat, Michael in the trunk. Paul rented a hotel room near the Wilkes-Barre/Scranton airport and he parked the car with the bodies still inside in the parking lot of the hotel, while he tried to reach Hugo.

Hugo was out of touch with Paul overnight. Paul was panicking and left with the bodies in his car.

Eventually, Hugo called back. The plan changed again. They would bury the bodies at the new house. Hugo went to the house and told Corvette Bob, still staying there, to leave for the day. He figured Hugo wanted him out of there for the day, so he left.

Hugo and Paul dug into the earth, choosing a low spot in the yard. They needed more dirt. Paul drove to Agway, an agricultural supply store in Dallas, and bought as many bags of dirt that would fill the car to the brim. He made more than a few trips to the store, filling the car each time to ensure they had enough potting soil.

When it was ready, they rolled the bodies out of the blankets and into the hole.

Michael went in first. Then Tammy.

The ties and tape stayed on.

The bodies were now covered in silence. Buried beneath the soil of the home at 479 Mount Olivet Road which Michael unknowingly had helped pay for—with his life.

CHAPTER 5

SHAKEDOWN

AFTER MICHAEL AND TAMMY VANISHED, Senior and Gerry Kerkowski were left spinning in the silence. They called Hugo. They were desperate, clinging to the hope that their son's closest friend could offer some clarity as to why they couldn't reach Michael.

But Hugo played dumb. Claimed he hadn't heard from Michael, didn't know about any travel plans.

The Kerkowskis got in touch with Lisa Sands, Tammy's sister. She said she hadn't heard from Tammy, but she wasn't too worried yet.

However, Tammy had mentioned that she was planning on returning home to take her son to Michael's son Connor's birthday party. When that day, a Saturday, came and went and she hadn't heard from Tammy, she became concerned. Lisa drove out to Michael's house and sat with the Kerkowskis that Saturday.

They waited, hoping that this was all some misunderstanding, that Michael and Tammy would walk through the door any minute. But despite Connor's planned birthday party, Michael never came.

Everyone drove back home and returned on Sunday. Still no call. No visit.

Finally, the Kerkowskis had no choice but to call the police.

Pennsylvania state trooper Mark Appleman responded. He walked through Michael's house with Gerry and Senior, took statements from them, and noted that the Kerkowskis hadn't moved a thing. They wanted investigators to see everything exactly as they had.

Appleman listened, and although he took the report seriously, his gut told him that Michael had run. Maybe to avoid sentencing. Maybe to regroup. Appleman talked with Michael's family and friends.

Appleman even called Hugo, whose tone was casual, dismissive. Hugo gave just enough to suggest the same theory: Michael had probably skipped town.

On May 14, 2002, Michael was set to be sentenced before Judge Vanston for his crimes. He never appeared. A warrant was issued for his arrest. He was declared a fugitive.

Weeks passed. Then months. Most people believed that Michael Kerkowski had amassed a lot of cash and fled the country with Tammy to avoid his legal troubles.

In July 2002, however, the silence was cracked.

A man who identified himself as Eric contacted Senior. Said he had information about Michael. Said he could help. Senior and Gerry arranged to meet this man in the parking lot of a doughnut shop in Dallas.

They entered his car, Senior in the front and Gerry in the back. The man formally introduced himself as Eric Sullivan. He told them that Michael was alive and had fled the country to avoid prison. And he claimed that for ten thousand dollars, he could contact Michael through untraceable means. The Kerkowskis told the man that they would think about it and contact him.

It sounded like madness. But in the couple's grief and uncertainty, even madness felt like hope.

The Kerkowskis left the meeting shaken, and they called Hugo for guidance.

Hugo told them not to give the man a dime.

Years later, "Eric Sullivan" would be identified as Paul Weakley. The man who had helped murder their son. His face was splashed across the television during his arrest.

Gerry saw it and told Senior, "My God, it's Eric Sullivan."

That same July, Hugo showed up at the Kerkowski home on Vine Street in Lehman Township again. He pulled Senior down to the basement and said Michael was still on the run, getting new lawyers and working on a new defense. But he needed money. Senior was concerned and confused but relieved to hear that his son was alive.

Senior handed over thirty thousand dollars. He did it because Michael had once said that he trusted Hugo more than his own lawyers and that Hugo was his best friend. As far as Senior knew, the only people who knew Michael had money at his parents' house were Senior, Gerry, and Michael. Hugo knew that Senior had been holding money for Michael. Senior believed Michael told Hugo about the money and to ask for it from them.

The Kerkowskis still had no proof that their son was alive, but they wanted to believe.

Later, Hugo added another layer of deception. He told Senior that Trooper Appleman had it out for the Kerkowskis—that he was threatening to charge them for lying for their son, that he'd said he was "going to nail their asses to the cross." This manipulation was meant to isolate the family from law enforcement, to quell any desire to go to the police again.

In one meeting with the Kerkowskis, as Hugo was talking, Gerry wrote on a napkin, "Is he alive?" and slid it to him. He looked at the napkin and smirked but didn't otherwise respond.

By August 2002, Hugo had returned to the Kerkowskis, saying that Michael needed more money. They reluctantly handed over another thirty thousand dollars. The questions kept coming. Why couldn't they talk to Michael? Why was Hugo the only messenger?

Weeks later, Hugo showed up again.

This time, the Kerkowskis demanded to speak with Michael. Hugo spent hours at the house, sitting with them on the back deck, pacing the backyard, pretending to be on the phone, nursing beers. Senior was growing more suspicious. Sensing something was amiss, he sent Gerry to the store to get her out of the house.

As it grew darker outside, Hugo and Senior went into the basement. Hugo sat on a couch, and Senior sat in his recliner. Senior told Hugo there would be no more money. Hugo's entire demeanor changed.

Hugo pulled out a gun.

"Your fucking life or the money," he said.

He fired the gun once—just over Senior's head and into the wall behind him. A warning. A terror tactic. Senior scrambled and collected another thirty thousand, fearful that Hugo might kill him and Gerry.

When Gerry returned home, Hugo was calm. He gathered his beer bottles in the basement, telling Senior he wasn't leaving any DNA, and marched Senior upstairs with a gun pressed to his back.

Gerry saw them emerge from the basement—Hugo close behind Senior, carrying a bag of clinking bottles that also contained another thirty thousand dollars. She didn't know what had happened.

Senior didn't tell her what had happened. In fact, he covered up the bullet hole in their wall with shoe polish so Gerry wouldn't see it. Senior was trying to figure everything out.

He lived in fear that Hugo would return for more money. Or worse.

To get clarity and in anticipation that Hugo would be back, Senior and Gerry made a list of five questions that only Michael would know how to answer.

- Where were you during the Agnes flood of 1972?
- What is the name of Connor's stuffed animal?
- Who was your date to your first prom?
- What is your maternal grandmother's name?
- Who took you to the Philadelphia hair show?

They were searching for proof of life. Something. Anything.

Hugo told them that the answers would be mailed to a relative's home in Swoyersville, Pennsylvania. The answers never appeared.

One of Hugo's associates, Pat Russin, was living on the Mount Olivet Road property at the time. He later testified that Hugo would drive by the Kerkowski home frequently.

One day, Hugo told Pat to get a package for him from the Kerkowskis. Hugo pulled into the driveway with Pat, gave him a phone, and kept another for himself. He called Pat's line and left it open so he could eavesdrop on what was said.

Pat went to the front door. Senior answered. Gerry stood behind him.

Pat said, "Hugo wants the package."

Senior replied, "I'm not giving him any more money," and handed him an envelope with the list of questions. "If you can answer these, we'll talk."

In September 2002, Hugo called Senior again. He wanted to meet—this time, at a McDonald's in Luzerne. He arrived with a friend who looked like he'd walked off the set of *Sons of Anarchy*. He was meant to look intimidating to Senior.

The friend, who had no idea what Hugo was up to or that he was being used as a prop of fear, went inside the McDonald's while Hugo pulled up next to Senior's car. Senior got into Hugo's truck.

Hugo leaned in and said he wanted the rest of Michael's money.

Senior said, "I think my son is dead. I'm going to the police."

Hugo turned dark. "Your house is on fire right now," he said. "And you've got another son."

Senior got out of the truck, saying, "I'm done with your lies and your bullshit."

That same day, he went to the police to report the shakedowns.

An investigation began that fall. The noose slowly tightened around Hugo, but the violence didn't stop.

On May 3, 2003, a year to the day after Michael and Tammy vanished from the face of the earth, Hugo showed up on the Kerkowskis' back porch. They wouldn't open the door. He later called the house and left a message: "It's not what it's usually about. He wants to talk to you. I guess you don't want to talk to me."

That message was vague but said so much and substantiated the Kerkowskis' story about being shaken down.

CHAPTER 6

THE RUDY AND REDMAN MURDERS

PAT RUSSIN EVENTUALLY CAME TO live on the Mount Olivet Road property with Hugo and Tina. He was crashing on the couch and helping around the property in exchange for a place to stay.

Tina would later say he was living out of a garbage bag. Russin was abusing drugs and spiraling out of control. He was also engaging in criminal activity to fuel his drug habit.

Hugo and Russin discussed a plan to lure drug dealers to the property and rob them. They identified two individuals, but that crime never materialized.

Hugo then invited two other reputed drug dealers, Frank ("Rudy") James, originally from New York City, and Adeiye ("Redman") Keiler, a native of Guyana, South America, over, under the pretense of turning his home into a drug operation. Russin figured that Hugo was looking for free drugs and intel or was going to rob Rudy and Redman.

On May 13, 2003, one year after the killing of Tammy and Michael, Hugo met up with the two men at Wilkes-Barre General Hospital and brought them back to Mount Olivet Road. The three of them and Russin sat around talking and eating pizza. Hugo and Russin eventually went inside.

While Rudy and Redman waited outside, Hugo asked Russin if he thought the men had money.

"I wanna whack 'em," Hugo said. Russin thought he was joking.

At some point, Russin fell asleep on the couch.

Hours later, around 1 a.m., he woke to see Hugo pacing, amped up. Hugo loaded three shells into a sixteen-gauge shotgun. He stepped outside, raised the weapon, and shot Rudy in the head. Rudy dropped instantly.

Redman took off running.

Hugo chased him around the garage, eventually cornering him and dragging him inside. Russin helped handcuff Redman and bind his legs with duct tape. Hugo handed Russin the shotgun and told him, "If he moves, shoot him."

Hugo returned to Rudy's body. Wrapped it in a tarp. Dragged it into the woods.

Later, Hugo took Redman to a bedroom upstairs. Then to the basement. Redman was still alive—shaken, tied, and confused.

In an eerie moment of faux camaraderie, Hugo told Redman he had no issue with him. He even asked him about other dealers they could rob. Then he said, "I'm starting to like this guy."

But it was all theater.

At dawn, Hugo brought Redman outside.

In the driveway, Hugo retrieved the shotgun and fired one round, hitting Redman. Then he yelled to Russin, "Get him! Grab him!"

Russin grabbed Redman's legs. Hugo fired again, this time into Redman's head.

They dragged the two bodies to a burn pit on the property. Wrapped them in tarps, stacked them with tires, and doused them in gasoline.

The fire burned for days.

Paul Weakley arrived a few hours later, early in the morning, and saw the flames. He walked over to the fire with the burning bodies, and the three men discussed the murders. He told Hugo they should bury the bodies.

Hugo refused. "Fuck burying them. We're burnin' 'em."

While the fire smoldered, Hugo left to attend a hearing regarding unpaid child support. Yes, child support.

Around 11 a.m. that day, he stood before Luzerne County judge Chester Muroski in a Luzerne County courtroom as the bodies continued to burn on his property.

For days, Hugo and Russin raked the fire pit, breaking bones, sifting ash.

Eventually, they shoved some of the remains into three garbage bags and stored them beside the house, a few feet from the pool.

CHAPTER 7

PAUL WEAKLEY'S CONFESSION

JUST AFTER THE RUDY AND Redman murders, the walls began closing in on Paul Weakley. He had committed and was being investigated for a series of local break-ins and church burglaries. Trooper Jerry Sachney of the Pennsylvania State Police was investigating him. He had also violated his federal probation, and a warrant for his arrest had been issued by the United States marshals.

Around that time, Officer Sam Blaski of the Kingston Police Department saw a silver minivan on Myers Lane parked suspiciously. He ran the vehicle registration and discovered that the vehicle was registered to Paul Weakley, who was wanted by the United States marshals.

Officer Blaski is "good police" and watched the vehicle for an hour and a half. He saw Weakley walk toward the vehicle, enter it, and begin driving toward his residence. Blaski followed the van and radioed Officers Rich Kotchik and Jeffrey Coslett for backup.

Weakley pulled onto Pulaski Street, where he lived, and headed toward his apartment. He backed into a parking stall but then suddenly threw the minivan into drive and took off again.

Weakley was acting as if he'd been alerted to Officer Blaski's presence. He drove aimlessly for a while as Blaski continued radioing with the other officers.

The officers initiated a traffic stop at the intersection of Grove and Division Streets. Weakley stopped his vehicle and was taken into custody without incident. Based on Weakley's history and proficiency in explosives, the officers searched the van for incendiary devices.

Weakley was taken back to police headquarters and searched. Officers found a handcuff key between his buttocks. They handed him over to a United States marshal.

Weakley's vehicle was searched and found to contain a black ski mask, rubber gloves, binoculars, wire cutters, garbage bags, and lighter fluid. Paul was arrested and held for a time and then placed on supervised release.

Ellen Smaka was Tina's best friend. She worked as a bartender at Dugan's Restaurant and Pub in Luzerne. Luzerne County District Attorney's Office detective Gary "Cap" Capitano frequented Dugan's. He came to know Ellen. She had been the victim of a home invasion and felt that the local police weren't doing enough. She asked Cap for help. Ellen suspected that Hugo and his associates had been involved in her robbery. She told Cap that her best friend was dating an ex-con named Hugo and she believed he and his associate Paul had victimized her.

Cap agreed to investigate Ellen's case, and he learned that trooper Jerry Sachney was looking into related cases. Cap and Sachney spoke and decided that they were going to interview Paul Weakley.

They interviewed him in early June 2003 over a few days.

On the morning of June 4, 2003, Paul Weakley, having been released by the marshals and placed back on supervised release, walked into the Luzerne County District Attorney's Office for a follow-up meeting. It was just after 9 a.m. He stepped up to the front desk and told the receptionist he had a meeting with Detective Gary Capitano.

He was holding a black gym bag and looked out of place in the lobby. Nervous. Eyes darting. Fidgeting. Cap came out to meet him and escorted him into the back offices.

Weakley was still gripping the bag. He told Capitano he wanted to hand something over. For a second, Cap thought there might be a bomb inside. Or worse, a head.

What Weakley handed over was a collection of burglary tools. The bag was filled with items he and Hugo Selenski had used during break-ins: surveillance gear, a handheld scanner, Motorola radios, jack wires, frequency guides, and even a black business folder. Cap inventoried the contents and turned the bag over to the Pennsylvania State Police.

Then came the real reason for the meeting. Paul knew his days were numbered. He knew the police were on his trail. He also knew that Hugo was out of control.

Weakley and Cap agreed to travel together to the state police barracks in Wyoming. There, inside an interview room, trooper Jerry Sachney joined Cap across the table from Weakley. Paul began to talk but his statements were self-serving and half-truths.

Paul began to tell Cap and Sachney the following:

Paul admitted that he and Hugo robbed Ellen. He told them that he'd met Hugo inside prison and that after his release, he lived with Hugo and Tina on Miller Street in Luzerne. He said everything changed the day Michael Kerkowski and Tammy Fassett went missing.

Paul originally lied to Sachney and Cap. He told them that Pat Russin and Hugo had actually killed Michael and Tammy on Friday, May 3, 2002. He claimed that they originally had buried their bodies near Dallas High School, and that Hugo had contacted Paul, asking for assistance in relocating the bodies from there to the Mount Olivet Road property.

Paul's confession was self-serving and insulating. He figured he could blame Pat Russin and Hugo and create a story that gave him the knowledge of how and where the bodies came to be on Hugo's property. He assumed that the investigators would find the bodies and buy his story.

Paul continued claiming that afternoon Hugo called him and made a strange request: rent a hotel room at the airport Holiday Inn Express. Paul was immediately suspicious. It wasn't just the request—it was Hugo's voice. He was pressing, specific. Paul later would say that Hugo instructed him to leave the key under the newspaper bin out front.

Paul asked why. Hugo said he had visitors from out of town and needed a quiet place to talk.

Paul complied. He rented the room, left the key where instructed, and returned to the house on Miller Street.

The next day, Saturday, Hugo called again. He wanted Paul to extend the room through Monday. This time, he said Pat Russin needed a place to stay, claiming Tina didn't want Pat in the house. Paul extended the reservation.

Then, on Sunday, May 5, 2002, Hugo made his first confession. Hugo told Paul that he and Pat Russin had killed Michael and Tammy and buried their bodies in the woods behind Dallas High School. They were in the car Hugo was using—Tina's white Honda Accord—when he said it.

Paul described that Hugo was high, mid-binge on cocaine, rambling, and agitated. He didn't give many details. Just that he and Pat had done it. And he wasn't happy with where the bodies were buried. He wanted them moved and didn't want Pat to know where they would end up.

Sachney asked, "What was your reaction?"

Paul said he was stunned. He couldn't believe Hugo had pulled him into something this dark. It was, he said, "the biggest thing I ever had to deal with in my life."

That night, around 8 or 9 p.m., Hugo asked Paul if he was ready to "do it." Paul stalled, suggesting they wait until later, when fewer people would be around. But eventually, he gave in.

Paul claimed that he and Hugo took separate cars: Paul drove in his 1995 Dodge Avenger, Hugo in the Accord. They drove behind Dallas High School, near the football fields. Hugo led them directly to the burial site. They started digging.

Paul said they didn't dig very deep. The bodies had been buried shallowly, wrapped in bedspreads. They dug just enough to expose them. Then they lifted the bodies out.

Paul described the tools they used: two short-handled green AMES spade shovels. He believed they'd bought them at Lowe's that Sunday. Hugo had accompanied him to the store.

Sachney, meticulous as ever, asked how the bodies had been positioned. Paul couldn't say. He remembered that they moved the female first, into the trunk of the Accord. When pressed, he couldn't recall the bedspread color but said that Tammy had been entirely wrapped. "I didn't see any part of her body," he said. "But I knew it was her. The other one was much heavier. Michael was a big guy."

He continued, saying that they loaded Michael's body next, into the Dodge.

Cap asked if they had flashlights.

"No."

Cap asked if he knew which way the feet had been facing—toward the flagpole or toward the stadium.

"No idea."

Paul said Michael weighed over 240 pounds. Tammy, maybe 130.

He told Cap and Sachney that they were back at the Miller Street house by 4:00 or 5:00 a.m. Hugo was wired on coke. Paul passed out. Paul claimed that Michael and Tammy remained in the trunks—one in the car in the driveway, the other in the car on the street.

Tina was home but asleep. Paul believed that Hugo took off again for more cocaine. "When he's on coke," he told Cap and Sachney, "he's a monster."

Paul woke around 7 a.m. on Monday. Hugo was gone. Paul called his cell phone but couldn't reach him. Eventually, Hugo called back.

He had a new plan.

He wanted to move the bodies to a property he and Tina were "investing in"—the Mount Olivet Road property.

Paul then described the burial of the bodies on Hugo's newly purchased property. He told Cap and Jerry where they put the bodies and that he had to go to the store to purchase potting soil.

He then said that an old hippie named Ernie Kulp, who lived in a trailer on the property, saw them digging. He asked what they were doing. Hugo said they were installing a fuel tank for ATVs.

In his initial statement Paul claimed that they cut the duct tape off the bedspreads and rolled the corpses into the hole. He claimed he couldn't remember who went in first. But he'll never forget what he saw next.

Michael was first. Then Tammy.

"I recognized her," Paul told Cap and Sachney. "It was the most hideous thing I've ever seen. Her face was black and swollen. It was bad. I still see it."

Both were clothed in jeans. Both were bound with zip cuffs on their wrists and ankles. Tammy had one around her neck. Paul assumed strangulation. But there was blood, too. "Lots of blood," he said.

He and Hugo buried them in a single grave, one on top of the other. Hugo did most of the digging.

Paul said he later took the bedspreads, duct tape, and soil bags to a car wash in Kingston. He vacuumed blood out of his car and handed the owner some cash to toss the bedding and trash into the dumpster.

In the interview, Cap asked Paul about the soil.

"It's not native to the area," Paul said. "I bought the better stuff—figured something should grow on it."

After the burial, Hugo gave Paul five thousand dollars to buy a van.

Cap asked Paul if it surprised him that Hugo had that kind of cash.

"No. Three weeks before the murders, Hugo came home with a shoebox filled with money," Paul told Cap and Sachey, adding that Hugo had told him he had been doing work for Michael—jury intimidation, mostly.

Cap asked where the murders had taken place.

Paul said Hugo told him that everything had happened on Friday, May 3, 2002, at Michael's home.

Paul then said he'd been inside the Kerkowski home twice. Once, just weeks before the murders. He waited in the car while Hugo went inside. He told Hugo that he didn't want to get involved.

But later, after the murders, Hugo brought him back. They tore apart the drop ceiling in the basement, searching for cash.

They found nothing.

Following Paul's interview, Paul rode with Cap, Sachney, and Pennsylvania State Police Sergeant Rick Krawetz in a state police van. They passed Hugo's Mount Olivet Road property three times.

Paul pointed out the concrete structure near where the bodies were buried. They also drove out to the dirt access road behind the Dallas High School football stadium. Paul said he remembered ambient light from the stadium the night they exhumed the bodies but couldn't pinpoint the burial site.

As the ride continued, Paul dropped one more bombshell.

He told the investigators that Hugo and Pat Russin had killed two more men three weeks prior—Black drug dealers named Rudy and Redman—at the Mount Olivet Road property.

He said their remains were likely still there—either in the burn pit or in a wheelbarrow. He said that Hugo had been putting some of their charred remains out for garbage as well.

Cap and Sachney, along with a team of investigators and assistant district attorneys, began working for hours on a warrant to search Hugo's property for the remains of Rudy, Redman, Michael, and Tammy.

CHAPTER 8

ALL THAT REMAINS ON MOUNT OLIVET ROAD

ON JUNE 5, 2003, A massive Pennsylvania State Police presence converged on the Mount Olivet Road property. Dozens of cars and forensic service vans entered the property with a search warrant.

When investigators arrived at the property, they zeroed in on the burn pit. Hugo was home at the time, and they handed him a copy of the warrant. They told him they were looking for buried bodies. He laughed and asked, "Is this a joke?" and said, "I'll help you dig."

Forensic experts and crime scene technicians moved in, digging slowly and deliberately. The work was tedious by design—measured in inches, not feet. Every scoop of dirt was sifted. Every bone fragment was cataloged.

Then they started finding them. Human bones.

The bones in the burn pit—charred black, smashed and brittle, fused with ash and soil—were believed to be the remains of Rudy and Redman.

There were pieces of clothing, such as zippers and metal buttons, from Snoop Dogg Jeans. There was even some human tissue located on a garage door, believed to have been deposited there after the shotgun blast to Redman.

It was a crime scene and a graveyard.

The team began to dig slowly and surgically into the area where Weakley had claimed Michael and Tammy were buried. As they dug, they noted that the potting soil was inconsistent with the dirt that was natural to the area, as Weakley had described. Then they saw a plastic flex tie jutting out of the ground.

The police first discovered Tammy Fassett's flex tie–bound feet and sneakers. They dug deeper and discovered her bound body atop Michael's body. Michael's hands were bound, and his decomposing face revealed duct tape across his eyes. The smell of decomposing flesh was wafting through the air.

The investigators were shocked and horrified. They brought in heavy digging equipment. Cadaver dogs were led through the property.

The media began to show up at the bottom of the property along the roadway. Word had been spreading of the massive police presence on the property. They went crazy, some referencing horror movies, making it all feel unreal.

But it wasn't fiction. It was Luzerne County. It was real.

When all was finished, the remains of at least five people were found on the Mount Olivet Road property. Two were quickly confirmed through dental records as Michael Kerkowski and Tammy Fassett.

The police brought in multiple agencies, people, and equipment to assist with the investigation: the FBI; the Bureau of Alcohol, Tobacco, Firearms and Explosives; the United States Attorneys' Office; the Pennsylvania Attorney General's Office; the Pennsylvania State Police; the Luzerne County Coroner's Office; Dr. Michael Baden; Dr. Lowell Levine; forensic dentists; anthropologists; cadaver dogs; and many more.

Police had found the remains of at least five people on Hugo's property. They removed many crushed bones that filled buckets. They had found Michael and Tammy and what they believed were the remains of Rudy and Redman. There were three left mandible jawbones in the burn pit. Which means there were at least three separate humans accounted for in the remains. Some anthropologists opined at the time that there could have been dozens of people in the pit, but the bones were smashed, burned, and discarded.

As I write, the identity of the fifth person remains unidentified.

Investigators remained on the property for over a month.

CHAPTER 9

THE JOURNEY BEGINS

PARDON ME, BUT THIS PART of the story case requires a little backtracking. In June 2003, I graduated from the Penn State Dickinson School of Law. I'd spent the previous three years living in Carlisle, just outside Harrisburg, with two of my closest friends, Michael "Deuce" Lombardo and Matthew "Goldie" Golden.

We shared a great apartment conveniently located between campus and the gym. I spent those years learning the law and working out. It was a good setup. Law school had its stressors, but I liked the grind.

I made lifelong friends. I found purpose. I spent my downtime at Blondie's bar, located a block away from our place. This was a happy time, and the whole world was ahead of us. Graduation came quickly, and it was time to return home to Luzerne County permanently.

I was packing up to move back home. The bar exam was looming, and I was neck deep in outlines, flash cards, and caffeine. That's when the news broke.

Back home in Luzerne County, a horror had been unearthed—literally. Human remains had been found on a property in Back Mountain. Bones.

Some charred, some completely burned. Some bound. The words in the headlines felt torn from pulp fiction: "pharmacist tortured," "bodies buried," "strangled," "dumped."

And at the center of it all was a name no one could stop repeating: Hugo Selenski.

A smiling, smirking ex-con. A man who made a spectacle of his own arrest, strutting proudly as officers led him in and out of court. At first, he was jailed and held only for threatening and assaulting Senior. That seemed to unravel everything else.

While I was studying for the bar exam, Luzerne County was becoming national news. Hugo's face was everywhere.

I studied and worked out for the next five weeks. Then it was time to take the Pennsylvania bar exam. There was a large digital clock at the front of the exam room. The exam was set to begin at 8 a.m. At 7:55 a.m., a proctor announced, "The Pennsylvania bar exam will begin in five minutes. Please take this time to prepare for the examination."

As I sat in this room with a few hundred prospective lawyers, I took those five minutes and said a quick prayer to my uncle Godfrey, whom I'd helped care for when I was growing up. I said silently, "I never asked you for anything. Help me get through this, and I will take care of people like you for the rest of my life."

In that brief moment, I could smell the cheap Old Spice aftershave that my uncle used to wear around me. I felt him with me and knew that I would be OK.

It would be months before the results were announced. Over the course of that summer and into the fall, more details of Hugo's case were being reported. I was following it very closely.

In August 2003, I began my first job as a law clerk for Lackawanna County judge Terrence Nealon. A law clerk position is a way to build your résumé and ease into the legal profession.

Judge Nealon was a gentleman and a fine judge, but it didn't take long before I became bored. I found myself tracking the Hugo Selenski case as if it were a second job—reading everything, watching every update, and memorizing names and movements.

Meanwhile, the investigation was proceeding. On October 6, 2003, Hugo and Pat Russin were officially charged with the murders of Frank "Rudy" James and Adeiye "Redman" Keiler.

Soon after the search of Hugo's property, Russin began to provide Cap and Jerry with evidence. He confessed to his role in the Rudy and Redman murders and what he knew about Hugo's many other crimes.

Then things became even wilder.

It was Friday, October 10, 2003. I was having dinner with Nicole and a group of friends at Gelpia'z restaurant in Kingston, just across the river from the county prison.

Anyone from Northeastern Pennsylvania remembers where they were that night. News broke across the TVs in the restaurant. The headline read: "Escape from Luzerne County Correctional Facility."

The waitress said it flatly, as if she were reading off the menu: "Hugo Selenski escaped."

We were glued to the televisions. Hugo had braided bedsheets into a rope, then pushed out a window that had been damaged for years and tossed a mattress out onto the yard. He used the mattress to climb over the razor wire fence.

Think about this for a second. It was 2003. A prisoner could tie bedsheets together to fashion them into a rope and slip down a wall.

It was cartoonish. It was real. And it worked.

Hugo had sent another inmate down first. That man fell and was badly injured. He later would claim that Hugo had shoved him.

Hugo didn't wait for the other prisoner. He chucked the mattress on top of the prison fence's razor wire and scaled the fence.

He was gone.

The news went national. There was a surreal sense of dread in the air. People locked their doors. The escape kicked off a three-day manhunt for Hugo. In the air, on the river, and in the woods, law enforcement searched everywhere. Ron Selenski Sr. pleaded on national television for Hugo to turn himself in. I remember checking the back seat of our car before we left the restaurant the night the news broke, just in case. Nicole was terrified. We went home and placed a chair under the doorknob of our small townhouse.

I told her, "I don't know why, but I have a weird feeling that this guy is going to become my problem." It was just intuition. I wasn't even a licensed lawyer yet, let alone a prosecutor.

He did, in fact, become my problem.

Hugo would later say that he never meant to escape and flee. Said it was just to prove he could.

It worked. He proved it. And that escape set the tone for everything that followed.

This wouldn't be a normal case. This wouldn't be routine.

Hugo wasn't a typical defendant. He was handsome, a manipulator. A showman. A narcissist with a God complex. And he was about to use the system like a stage.

On October 13, 2003, Hugo eventually turned himself in from his home at Mount Olivet Road. He negotiated a peaceful surrender through his attorney, Demitrius "Tim" Fannick.

Tim Fannick was tall and articulate. He had pleaded on national television for Hugo to turn himself in. Like Hugo, Fannick was also becoming well-known from the case.

Hugo was back in jail. Investigators later learned that after his escape, he had traveled along the river to Pittston. From there, he moved through a nearby neighborhood and arrived at his aunt's house. She was frightened, but he stayed there for a short time. Eventually, she drove him to an area near Mount Olivet Road, where he continued on foot back to his home. Law enforcement had already searched the residence and were still canvassing the area, but he somehow managed to slip past them.

The same week that Hugo turned himself in, I found out that I had passed the Pennsylvania bar exam.

I continued on in my clerkship. However, in early 2004, I wanted a change and decided it was time to become a prosecutor. I applied for an open position at the Luzerne County District Attorney's Office. In March 2004, I was called for an interview.

My interview was with District Attorney Dave Lupas and First Assistant Jackie Musto-Carroll. I was immediately comfortable with them. I felt very much at home in their presence. They would become mentors and friends.

I told myself, *Don't mention the Hugo case.* But of course, I did.

Lupas laughed. "Don't worry," he said. "You won't have to deal with that case."

But he was wrong. It just took a while.

They offered me a job during my interview. On April 4, 2004, I was sworn in by Judge Joseph Augello. Lupas and Musto-Carroll stood with me. My mom and Nicole held the Bible as I took my oath.

At that time, Hugo was locked down in a special cell at SCI Dallas. I felt a pulse in my chest. Purpose. For the first time, I wasn't just a lawyer—I was a prosecutor. My life was about to change.

The first prosecution was for the murders of Rudy and Redman. That case wandered through the courts for nearly three years, a slow march of motions and delays. Hugo was an accused murderer but he remained a local spectacle.

The press ran endless features on Hugo's so-called celebrity, the circus of it all. I remember that one article showed off his jailhouse artwork and even quoted him calling out members of our office by name.

My brothers teased me about it over one Sunday dinner. They said, "This Hugo guy is calling out lawyers in your office, and you're not mentioned."

I fired back, half joking, half burning: "I'd shut that guy up."

Truth was, it was killing me. I wanted to be in the fight. But I had no business being there yet. I was still a rookie. I hadn't earned it.

March 2006 came, and Hugo finally stood trial for Rudy and Redman's murders. I'd slip into the courtroom gallery when I could, watching from the back row, silently wishing I were part of the team.

Assistant District Attorney Jim McMonagle, joined by Christopher O'Donnell and Sam Sanguedolce—all good men and fine prosecutors—led the prosecution. Jim was removed from Gacha to lead this team. But Defense Attorney Tim Fannick, sharp and relentless, was putting on a show with Hugo by his side.

The media hammered the District Attorney's Office after the escape, in the pretrial hearings and during the trial. The office was looking outmatched. I had a bad feeling in my gut that Hugo was going to beat the case.

The media had platformed Hugo. He would have lines of people waiting to watch the court proceedings. There were women writing to him, enamored with Hugo, the arrogant bad boy. The

District Attorney's Office was limited in how it could respond to such accounts in the press. There are rules that apply to prosecutors. The way to respond was in the courtroom. The District Attorney's Office was falling short there too.

I met with Dave Lupas in his office and offered to start prepping a Plan B—a backup strategy in case the trial went sideways. I told myself I was being overly dramatic, hoping I was wrong. I wasn't.

Lupas was becoming concerned about the office's chances as well, and a day or so later called a meeting with Musto-Carroll, Assistant District Attorney Dave Pedri, Cap, Sachney, and me. He expressed concern and said, "Let's develop a plan in the event we lose the case."

While the trial for the Rudy and Redman murders played out upstairs in the courtroom, we were prepping in our office downstairs for the other murder case involving Hugo. Cap gave us the original warrant and a draft arrest affidavit for the murders of Michael and Tammy. We spent a few days finalizing the paperwork, and Plan B was in place.

March 15, 2006. The jury went out and then came back with the verdict.

Hugo Selenski is not guilty of murder.

The courtroom erupted. Chaos in every corner. Reporters scrambled; whispers turned into gasps. Hugo Selenski had just been acquitted of the charges of murdering Rudy and Redman.

The verdict appeared to be the result of some jury confusion. The reason didn't matter, however; they acquitted Hugo. Our office lost, and Hugo had won. He was actually convicted of a much lesser charge of abuse of a corpse, which would carry no additional jail time.

He was "not guilty" in this case, but he wasn't going to walk free.

Plan B had to be put into action. Hugo was going to be arrested for the murders of Michael and Tammy. I entered the courtroom and watched as detectives and state police surrounded him, executing Plan B. Without missing a beat, they arrested Hugo for the murders of Michael Kerkowski and Tammy Fassett.

The police marched Hugo out of the courthouse and over to the Pennsylvania State Police barracks in Wyoming for processing.

I jumped into Cap's detective car. Cap was driving. He was angry and heartbroken. He had just lost the biggest case of his career. Cap was stubborn, proud, disciplined, and tough. I had spent only a short time in his company as we prepared the new charges, but I was already starting to like him.

I said, "I know this is bad, Cap, but I promise we will get this guy together."

He looked at me and said, "Shut the fuck up, kid," and kept driving. So, I did as he asked and shut up.

News cameras and members of the media followed our convoy. Flashbulbs popped as we pulled into the barracks. I entered the barracks and saw Hugo sitting cuffed to a bench, silent. He looked up at me. His eyes flickered. He was confused and clearly frustrated. When our eyes locked, I felt like Hugo was sizing me up as a new face to this craziness.

Here sat this five-foot-ten, normal-looking man who had created such chaos.

After officers processed him, they led Hugo out to another convoy of police vehicles, and we traveled to the office of Judge James Tupper, where Hugo was going to be formally arraigned on the new charges.

Some media followed other members of the press camped out when we arrived. Dave Pedri and I made our way into the small courtroom and sat down at the prosecution table. Lupas and Musto-Carroll were handing in the paperwork.

Pedri and I were sitting at the prosecution table. Hugo sat at the defense table alone but surrounded by troopers.

Pedri asked me, "What happens now?"

I whispered, in a joking tone, "I don't know. I've never been to a homicide arraignment."

Hugo sat quietly, taking in all this madness. He was arraigned, and we left the office. The media swirled outside. We had taken the first step of what would become a decade-long journey. I was ready, or at least I thought so.

That weekend, we brought the Kerkowskis into the District Attorney's Office. They were shattered—grief now twisted with fury. This was the first time I met the Kerkowskis. We all sat around a table, and I could sense their anger toward Lupas and their disappointment. The man they believed had killed their son had been acquitted of two murders.

It was a strange meeting, to say the least. Cap was clearly angry and uncomfortable as well. No one said much.

Lupas said that he was forming a new prosecution team to handle Michael's case. He introduced Musto-Carroll, Pedri, and me to the Kerkowskis. I remember the two of them staring at me. I looked back at them and tried to send a nonverbal message of calm.

We assured the Kerkowskis that Hugo would not slip away this time and that this new team would bring him to justice. However, they appeared doubtful—and rightfully so. After the meeting, I walked them out into the hallway. As they were leaving,

I said, "This time will be different. I promise you both." Gerry said thank you and that she hoped I was right.

Pedri and I got to work that week. We organized thousands of pages, hours of recordings, lists of witnesses.

We built a war room outside the courthouse because we feared someone inside was leaking information to the press. Paranoia was warranted. We worked with Lupas, Musto-Carroll, Cap, and Sachney as we developed the case. Michelle Giza was our trial assistant. As we were preparing for a preliminary hearing, Dave and I would draft questions for witnesses and memos on the law. We were third- and fourth-chair prosecutors on the case at this point, but I didn't care. I just wanted in on the case.

I began to secure and read copies of the police reports, totaling thirty thousand pages, and to organize the case. I spent the next twelve months in the war room or at my kitchen table with blue binders and eventually a laptop computer with the entire case file. The case became my passion—my job and my hobby.

Everything else in my life felt like a distraction from the file, and I would spend hours reading and writing. I was amazed and horrified as I learned who Hugo was and what he had done. I would fall asleep with a binder in my hand. Sleep became sporadic. I would wake up and go downstairs to the kitchen table in the middle of the night and just keep reading.

Hugo was on my mind twenty-four/seven. I remember being out socially with friends in those early days, and I would just get lost in my thoughts. It was a darkness I carried everywhere I went.

I felt like Hugo was in his cell, readying himself for what would be our showdown. He had nothing else to do, and I had all of these distractions. I began to physically train more intensely, too. I continued to work out and began running.

I converted countless hours of Hugo's prison visit and phone recordings that we were monitoring from the prison to audio files playable on my phone and listened to them while I ran. I knew that in order to understand and prosecute Hugo successfully I had to know what he was thinking.

I wanted this fight. Hugo used to refer to himself as the "Big Bad Wolf." It was incomprehensible to me that every prosecutor in the office wouldn't have been fighting for this case.

I came to know the Kerkowskis well over the next several months. We would meet regularly and discuss the case. We would assure them that our team was working hard and preparing. We would prepare their testimony for the preliminary hearing.

I also met Lisa Sands, Tammy's sister, along with Ashley Owen, Tammy's niece. They were a loving family who had also been ripped apart by this murder.

Tammy was a country girl who'd gotten caught up in this mess. Lisa and Ashley were always present in our case and would meet with us regularly as well.

Weakley had stopped cooperating with investigators. As Cap and Sachney reviewed all the evidence, they confirmed that Pat Russin had an alibi for the murders of Michael and Tammy. Further examination of records and evidence revealed that Paul hadn't merely helped move the bodies. He had participated in the murders of Michael and Tammy alongside Hugo.

Paul Weakley was eventually arrested and charged with the killings of Michael and Tammy as well. He and Hugo were also charged with counts of conspiracy. This meant that they had to be brought into court and told of the new charges in an arraignment. I remember being in the same room as the two men for the first time. Paul had been the one who blew the whistle on Hugo, so you can imagine Hugo wasn't happy to see him.

In their presence, Hugo looked deep into your eyes, but it felt like Weakley looked through your eyes and into your soul. He was pale and lean, standing only five foot nine. I had read so much about him in the previous weeks. I knew neither of them was to be trifled with or taken lightly at any point.

In August 2006, we had a preliminary hearing on the charges against Hugo and Weakley. Gerry and Senior testified to everything: they talked about Hugo's involvement with Michael, how they'd found the house, and the shakedowns.

At one point during the preliminary hearing, Hugo was smiling at Gerry as she was testifying, and she lashed out at him. The charges were bound over to court, meaning the judge had found enough evidence to believe that a crime had been committed. We would be moving on to trial.

The case was filed as a capital case. Meaning Hugo and Paul would face the death penalty if convicted. The case qualified as a death penalty case because Hugo and Paul tortured Michael, killed more than one person, had histories of violent felonies and the killings were done in the course of a robbery.

Then, out of nowhere, on September 9, 2006, Senior died suddenly of a heart attack at his home. Undoubtedly, the stress of losing his son and the pressures he faced led to his death. This was horrible news. Not only was Senior a good man, and this was another tragedy for Gerry, but he was intended to be a key witness in our case.

I was preparing for the Joseph Gacha trial in September 2006 as well. The trial would be later that month. So I had to put down the Hugo file for a bit and focus on Gacha for the murder of Carrie Martin.

Nicole and I were expecting our first child any day, too. I was getting used to this fast-paced life.

Lupas, Musto-Carroll, Pedri, Cap, Michelle Giza, and I all went to Senior's wake together to personally express our condolences to Gerry and her family. We walked into the funeral home and stood in line. I could feel the family staring at us. Pedri, Musto-Carroll, and Cap were ahead of me, and they hugged Gerry as she cried.

I approached Gerry and gave her a hug. Still crying, she took my hand and led me closer to the casket. She said to me, "This is Hugo's latest victim. Jarrett, Mike [Senior] died of a broken heart. He trusted you. He believed in you."

She told me she had no reason to go on but to see justice for her son and now her husband, too.

She continued, "Promise me right here and now you are going to get him no matter what."

I said, "I swear to you right here, we will get him together." She squeezed my hand and gave me a look that said she was leaving it to me.

In October 2006, my son, Dominick, was born. I transferred to being a part-time assistant district attorney, but nothing about the job was part-time. I joined my law firm with Bill Finnegan. Lupas added former Assistant District Attorney Mike Melnick to our team. Melnick was a grizzled former prosecutor whom Cap insisted be brought back to be part of our team. He was eccentric and old school. He was a legend in the District Attorney's Office. He used to call me "bulldog," which I loved. He helped develop our strategy for the Hugo case and was a source of humor in those years as well. I prosecuted many other murderers over the decade it took for Hugo's trial to begin. But Hugo was always there. Watching. Waiting. And I couldn't shake the feeling that he and I were connected. As if we were carrying the same dark truth, one that had to be dragged into the light no matter how long it took.

During that time, I worked to earn the trust of our witnesses. Hugo was playing games from behind bars, leading to what would be an almost ten-year delay.

Motions. Hearings. Appeals. Legal footwork that kept the trial from ever really starting. Hugo fired attorneys. Claimed bias. Demanded a change of venue. Accused prosecutors of misconduct.

The system bent under the weight of it. And all the while, Gerry and Lisa waited. They waited through the hearings and public fights. Through the press. Through the rumors. Through the silence. Hugo remained a media darling, gracing the covers of the local papers every time we were in court.

As the case lingered, Gerry broke down in a meeting with Cap and me one day. She was tired. Hurt. Furious that Hugo was on every front page like some kind of celebrity.

"Why does he always get such attention?" she asked. "Why does the media take his picture and treat him like a movie star? He tortured my son."

I said, "I don't know. But when this is over, they are going to take a picture of you and me."

She smiled and said, "I hope you're right."

CHAPTER 10

CHANGING OF THE GUARD

IN SPRING 2007, THE HUGO Selenski case was still sitting in the limbo of the appellate court. Progress had stalled. The case had momentum but no runway.

Lupas sat our team down and told our team that he was running for judge.

He and Musto-Carroll had been leading the prosecution team, but Pedri and I had drawn the blueprint of this case. The engine was still humming. Musto-Carroll was stepping up to run for district attorney, and I had every bit of confidence in her.

Lupas won his judgeship. Musto-Carroll entered the DA race against Defense Attorney Vito DeLuca. It was a clean, respectful campaign.

Jackie Musto-Carroll was an easy candidate to support—sharp, prepared, and poised to be the first female district attorney in Luzerne County history. She was also my friend. She coasted into the seat, and our new team was locked in place. The attorneys were Musto-Carroll, Mike Melnick, Pedri, and me. The investigators remained Cap and Jerry Sachney, and the District Attorney's Office case manager Michelle Giza was still assisting.

Things were calm on the surface, but we knew the storm would eventually come.

At that point, attorney John Pike was representing Hugo, with help from Michael Senape, Robert Butner, and David Lampman.

The legal chessboard was set up. We just didn't know how long the match would last.

Friday-morning meetings became a ritual: coffee, sarcasm, planning for months and years. We'd break down our task lists, check progress, make plans. The pressure hadn't yet peaked. The case was still on appeal. We had space to think and refine.

That was my moment to sharpen the blade. To dial in every detail of how we'd eventually bring Hugo to trial.

Musto-Carroll would correct us when we called him "Hugo."

"He's not your friend," she'd say. "He's nobody special. He's the defendant."

I knew that. But Hugo wasn't just another name on a case file. He wasn't like the rest. I didn't call him "Hugo" out of friendship or respect—I called him that because I wanted to remember exactly who I was dealing with.

And the sooner everyone else understood that he wasn't like the rest, the better off we'd all be.

Weakley's confession, or half confession, fell apart. After many conversations, he eventually acknowledged his role in the murders of Michael and Tammy and agreed to plead guilty in federal court to killing them. He was going to serve life in prison and testify against Hugo in our case. In exchange, we took the death penalty off the table. Weakley eventually came clean to Detective Lieutenant Dan Yursha of the District Attorney's Office. Yursha was a close friend of Cap's and brought on to assist with the case. Yursha was sharp and would disarm people with his charm. Weakley didn't want to give Cap or Sachney the satisfaction of his confession and he seemed to have a rapport with Yursha.

Around this time, I began meeting with Paul Weakley along-side our team. Having studied him extensively, it felt surreal to finally get to know him in person. We often met at whichever jail he was being held in, or he was transported to the District Attorney's Office for our discussions. I remained cautious around Paul, but he was both intriguing and surprisingly funny. Over the years, we shared many conversations and lunches, and I came to know him well. He was never shy about sharing his opinions or discussing his views on the world.

On June 13, 2008, Weakley pleaded guilty to his federal charges. I sat in the courtroom with Gerry and Lisa and our team. During the sentencing, Gerry said to Weakley, "I wish you could see inside my body to see what a broken, demolished heart really looks like. You will never in a million years know the pain, the heartache, the stress, and the anguish you have caused my family. Michael was my firstborn, and he was everything to me and my husband."

Lisa Sands showed pictures of Tammy to Weakley. She said to look closely at the loving young woman, mother, daughter, sister, and friend to everyone.

Lisa said that Tammy was not only her sister but her best friend. She said, "If our family had our way, you or Hugo wouldn't be safe anywhere.... You animals don't deserve to live on earth."

Paul apologized to Gerry and Lisa. He said, "I am not asking for forgiveness. I want you to know I am truly sorry."

CHAPTER 11

THE CASTLE CRUMBLES

FROM 2007 TO 2010, THE Selenski case sat in the appellate courts, stalled in legal purgatory. The first delay came from our effort to admit a robbery that Paul and Hugo committed in the nearby Pocono Mountains. Weakley told Cap that he and Hugo broke into a jeweler named Samuel Goosay's home and had tied him up with flex ties and duct tape as they had done to Michael. Hugo remained with the Goosay and Paul traveled to the jewelry store to rob it. The alarm was tripped and the robbery was botched. Goosay managed to see through a portion of the duct tape after a struggle with Hugo. He saw Hugo's face and was able to identify him eventually.

Our team argued that the crime—specifically, the use of flex ties and duct tape on a business owner inside their home, committed by Paul and Hugo—constituted a signature offense. I believed the Goosay robbery would serve as powerful evidence against both Hugo and Paul in our prosecution. However, the court denied our motion to admit this critical signature evidence, leading us to file an immediate appeal. That appeal remained pending for several years, causing the initial delays in the case.

During those years, life moved forward. I was settling into fatherhood and married life and building out my private practice. I became a partner and then a named partner in our law firm.

Business was strong. My law partner Paul Pugliese would needle me about my "twenty-dollar-an-hour job" at the DA's office, pointing out that I was losing money by staying on.

He wasn't wrong. But I didn't care.

I'd found a way to balance both lives—earning for my family while holding onto the job that meant so much to me. The courtroom still pulled at me in ways that private practice never could.

Musto-Carroll was assigning me homicide after homicide. Many of the other prosecutors didn't like that I was getting the big cases. I didn't expect them to. I wasn't there to win a popularity contest. I was there to prosecute.

And prosecute I did.

I put Joseph Gacha away for murdering Carrie Martin. Alongside Pedri, I secured convictions against Alan Leitzel and Tiffany Simmons for killing baby Xavier. I convicted Donnell Buckner of killing Kewaii Rogers Buckner.

I prosecuted a man who hacked his girlfriend to death with a hatchet. I secured a conviction against a gang member who executed a rival female drug dealer in broad daylight.

Each case was its own battle—teaching me, sharpening me, preparing me for the day I'd face Hugo in trial.

I treated all of my cases like a prize fight, approaching each with rigorous discipline. I would read the files and reread the rules of evidence and procedure. I would eat less in the weeks leading up to a trial to slim down. I would physically train, spending hours at the gym in a six-week training camp. The physical aspect of my preparation built my confidence in the courtroom.

But as my teams and I built cases, the courthouse was cracking.

The rumors started slowly in 2008. FBI warrants. Whispered names. Judges. Attorneys. County workers. The feds were closing in, and it wasn't long before the whole rotten foundation buckled.

Judge Michael Conahan from Hazleton, long suspected of keeping the wrong kind of company, rose to become president judge. He and Mark Ciavarella, a Wilkes-Barre native and juvenile court judge, became close.

Then in January 2009, it dropped: the feds charged both with accepting $2.6 million in kickbacks to green-light a private juvenile detention center.

The scandal exploded: "Kids for Cash."

And they weren't the only ones going down. By the end, more than thirty public officials were charged. Court administrators. Judges. Lawyers. School board members. Police officers. Corruption had seeped into every corner of Luzerne County's government.

The courthouse didn't just take a hit; it was gutted.

Everyone was looking over their shoulders. Even those who weren't charged had been interrogated or flipped for cooperation. You could feel the panic clinging to the walls.

The corruption and ensuing scandal deeply shook my faith in the system. It shattered my confidence in the courts and the courthouse itself. I became increasingly concerned about how we could move forward with one of the largest cases in Luzerne County's history amid what many were calling the most corrupt courthouse in the nation. I knew the situation was dire, but I also recognized that many good, dedicated people remained in place even after the corruption arrests and trials.

Musto-Carroll was up for reelection as district attorney. Typically, a second term for a district attorney was a foregone conclusion, but these were strange times.

Shockingly, she lost her reelection bid in 2011 to a young attorney named Stefanie Salavantis. We were all together watching the results roll in.

Cameras flashed. No one spoke. My head was spinning—not from politics, but from knowing that our team had just been shattered.

Two days later, we were back in court for a status conference on Hugo. The courtroom was packed. Musto-Carroll was composed, but her energy had changed.

She and Hugo were communicating through intermediaries. He was going to be requesting a delay for new counsel. This delay would push the case past Musto-Carroll's term.

I was standing near Hugo before the judge that day. He leaned toward me and said, "Last man standing, eh, Ferentino?"

I smiled, even as something in me cracked. "Hugo," I said, "when this is over, I'll be the last man standing."

He didn't like that.

His eyes shifted. Cold. Calculating. I could see a vein in the side of his head become prominent. I have heard others describe that vein when Hugo gets angry. He said, "A lot of people thought that."

And just like that, the match was set—or so I thought.

In Musto-Carroll's final days, Salavantis sent letters encouraging members of the office to remain on board. Pedri and I did not receive a letter. It was clear that he and I were supporters of Musto-Carroll's and would not be welcome in the new administration.

I was devastated but understood that's how the system works. I wouldn't be able to see the Hugo case through, and I would break my promise to Gerry Kerkowski. That's what hurt the most. I wasn't going down without a fight.

I had a family to support. We were expecting a second child. That night, I sat alone at the kitchen table—the same table where I had prepped many hours for the Selenski case. And I knew I wasn't done. Hugo and I still had unfinished business, and I had a promise to keep.

I requested a meeting with Salavantis.

We sat down in December 2011. She was polite but cautious. I knew the whisper campaigns had gotten to her, warning her that I was too tied to Musto-Carroll.

I acknowledged supporting Musto-Carroll and that we were friends, but made something else very clear: this wasn't about politics. This was about justice. About finishing what we started.

Cap and others from the state police put in a word for me, too. I assured Salavantis that if she were to keep me on the team, I would earn her trust and not hurt her.

Days later, a letter arrived. The same letter that had shown up in everyone else's mailbox. I'd earned my seat back at the table. I called Salavantis to thank her and wished her a Merry Christmas.

A few days later, I met with Salavantis and Sam Sanguedolce for lunch. Sanguedolce had supported Salavantis and was going to be her first assistant.

Salavantis said she was going to be putting Sanguedolce in as lead on the Hugo case, but that I was going to be able to stay on. I didn't care who was leading or where I sat, so long as I was at the table. We agreed on one thing: it was time to rebuild.

We met again in the war room a few days later. Salavantis and Sanguedolce joined the rest of us. I ran through a forty-five-minute presentation—every fact, every angle. I wanted them to see the depth. The work. The absolute command of what we were up against.

That was the start of something new.

Dave Pedri, one of my closest friends and my partner in the District Attorney's Office, had left when Musto-Carroll's administration ended. I was sad to see him go, but he went on to become the county solicitor and county manager.

I was happy for Pedri and the success he found after leaving the District Attorney's Office. We remain very close friends.

Mike Melnick left as the case lingered on as well.

So we had to build a new prosecution team.

"If there is no enemy within," the proverb goes, "the enemy outside can do me no harm."

Sanguedolce and I worked well together. He let me argue. Let me cross-examine witnesses instead of just scripting the questions. We gave each other space to be who we were. He, too, had a score to settle with Hugo from the first trial. And that made us dangerous together.

We then added Assistant District Attorney Mamie Phillips to our team. Phillips was and is a dear friend, a tough prosecutor who fears no one. I knew that she would be a tremendous asset to our team. She was to handle all the evidence-collection witnesses and allow Sam and me to focus on the major fact witnesses.

In July 2012, Nicole and I welcomed our baby girl, Victoria. Becoming a girl dad has been one of the most amazing experiences of my life. As our family grew the Hugo case meandered through the system due to legal challenges, judicial and representation changes.

In those years, I would get so immersed in the case that I would have nightmares of Hugo and Paul coming into my home. I would wake up thinking about an aspect of the case and couldn't fall back to sleep. I would go for long runs and get lost in my thoughts and occasionally on the run. I was obsessed but knew in my heart that this case required a little unhealthy obsession.

In 2015, the waiting was over. The commonwealth was ready. After the judicial scandals, we were assigned our possibly tenth and final judge to preside: Judge Fred Pierantoni, a former assistant district attorney, a longtime local magistrate, and a fellow Greater Pittston native. I knew he would be a fair and no-nonsense judge. He would go on to prove to be just that.

And this time, Hugo wouldn't be able to lawyer his way out.

After years of delays—false starts, restarts, promises of trial that never materialized—we were finally at the brink. I'd seen more trial dates evaporate than I cared to count.

Over a dozen defense attorneys had come and gone. Ten judges had taken their turn on the bench. Witnesses had died, including Senior and Ernie Culp. Our prosecution team had been built up, torn down, and rebuilt.

The media had circled for years, politicians had circled for gain, and through it all, we'd endured. Now, this was the moment.

I felt it, lightning in my veins. Not adrenaline. Not nerves. Purpose.

I was ready. This wasn't a burden to me. It was a fight I welcomed. Our team was ready too.

In Pennsylvania, you are not allowed to have cameras in the courtroom to video or photograph proceedings. I had arranged for a sketch artist to be in the courthouse the first day of trial. I expected one would be there, but I wanted my own to capture the trial. I wanted Hugo to feel it—to know that I was so certain of this moment, I wanted it immortalized. I walked the artist to his seat in the courtroom, the one I'd made sure was positioned perfectly.

I turned and said, loudly enough for Hugo to hear: "When I am delivering the opening and you draw the picture, make sure Hugo and I are in it."

Hugo caught it. Looked up and said, "You brought this guy?"

I didn't flinch. "Yes, I am going to hang this picture in my office someday."

He laughed nervously and said, "You're something, Ferentino."

That's exactly what I wanted. For him to feel that this wasn't just another trial. This was the reckoning. I wanted him to see I wasn't intimidated by the moment, by him, or by the weight of the case.

I looked at him for a moment and thought, *I wonder if he knows how much I love what I'm about to do to him.*

I had lived with it, trained with it, and welcomed the fight. I was proud of what my team and I had built. And I knew—we all knew—the victory was coming. And I would relish every second of it. It was time to respond to the media puff pieces on Hugo and all of the shade cast on our office after the first loss. It was time to keep my promise to Gerry, Cap, and myself too.

On January 21, 2015, after beginning as a fourth-chair seated member of the team, I was about to deliver the opening statement in the Hugo Selenski trial.

As the judge instructed the jury, I said a quiet prayer to my late father and late uncle. I asked them not for victory but for the strength to get through the trial.

I stood and said to the jury, "We are about to go on a journey. It's a journey that I have been waiting nine years to take you on. It's a journey into the world of Hugo Selenski, a world of violence and greed. It's a world that leaves its victims bound and broken. What you will hear will shock you, it will horrify you, and it will break your heart."

I spoke for seventy-two minutes straight. I told the jury the story and watched their horror and heartbreak. I introduced the parties and cast of characters. I laid out the road map of our case. I told them about the flex ties and the lust for money over life.

I told them that the check Tina wrote for the house had cleared, and I told them that Michael and Tammy had been rolled into the hole like dogs. I said, "You wouldn't give an animal a grave like that."

Every word I spoke was laced with vengeance. Gerry and Lisa watched from the gallery, and I wanted them to see that we weren't afraid, and that this time it was Hugo's throat we were going for.

I told the jury, "The defense will blame Weakley for everything. They will show he's a liar and killer." I told the jury, "The worse Weakley looks, remember one thing: we didn't bring him here. He's here because Hugo brought him here to northeast Pennsylvania, because he's all of those things, and now he wants to shield himself with the very attributes that made Weakley his partner in crime."

Weakley took the stand, and I questioned him. He'd spent many hours with our team preparing his testimony in the years leading up to the trial.

He was a criminal for sure, but he was also funny and very bright.

I had a rapport with Weakley. I needed him to trust me. We built that trust, and it allowed him to become a better witness. His deal with the government still rankled many, but his testimony was surgical. He was dressed in a gray suit and wore glasses on the stand. We joked together that he looked like an accountant.

He walked the jury through the timeline. The method. The burial. He never looked at Hugo. He barely blinked. The man who had once buried bodies now buried his partner with words.

Gerry Kerkowski's day to testify came, too. We were sitting together in the conference room before she took the stand. Connor—her grandson and Michael's son, now a seventeen-year-old young man—accompanied her.

I held her hand and said, "It's just you, me, and him [Hugo] up there. This is what you've been waiting for."

She said, "This is what I have been living for."

Her health had been deteriorating. She'd had some close calls recently. She told me that she wasn't going anywhere until she saw Hugo convicted.

She took the stand and did amazing. She told her and Senior's story, and when the time came to identify Hugo, I said, "Do you see Mr. Selenski here today?" Hugo leaned forward and proudly smiled.

Gerry said, "Take that smile off of your face." The judge banged his gavel, but the message was clear: the end of Hugo's smiling days was upon us.

Our team ran like a well-oiled machine. Sanguedolce handled many legal arguments and questioned Tina Strom and Pat Russin, among others. He delivered a powerful closing argument that served to summarize and reinforce our case.

Attorneys Bernard Brown, E.J. Rymsza, and Hugh Taylor led the defense. They countered with doubt.

They painted Weakley as the real killer. Said Hugo was a manipulator, yes, but not a murderer. They cited the absence of DNA, inconsistencies in Weakley's lies and stories. They said Hugo was being railroaded by a desperate system trying to fix its own failures.

But the jury wasn't buying it.

We presented thirty witnesses over a two-week span. The defense called a dozen witnesses. The jury deliberated for twelve hours over a day and a half.

Then it happened. The jury reached a verdict.

Our team marched into the courtroom. Sanguedolce and I walked over to Gerry and her supporters to tell them the jury had reached a verdict. Judge Pierantoni took the bench and confirmed that the jury had indeed come to a decision. The jury foreperson handed the verdict to the judge's clerk, who passed it to the judge. After reviewing it, Judge Pierantoni returned the document to the jury and instructed the foreperson to read the verdict aloud.

"We, the jury, find the defendant, Hugo Marcus Selenski, guilty of the murder of Michael Kerkoski, guilty of the murder of Tammy Lynn Fassett."

They continued reading the remaining charges, but to be honest, I didn't hear anything after that.

I stared over at Hugo, and he stared back. We said nothing. I was overcome. I felt tears fall from my eyes and actually heard them hit the wooden table. I put my hand on Cap's shoulder as the foreperson continued to read the jury's verdict.

Our team was exhausted. Everyone had done an amazing job.

Hugo Selenski had finally been convicted. Long referred to as "accused murderer Hugo Selenski" became "convicted murder Hugo Selenski."

The Hugo Selenski prosecution team had many manifestations over the years. Everyone made their own contributions. The prosecution and conviction were truly a team effort and I do not attempt or intend to suggest otherwise.

CHAPTER 12

THE NIGHT IT ENDED

WHEN THE VERDICT FINALLY CAME in, everyone except me headed to Dugan's Pub in Luzerne to celebrate. I had been planning to have a celebratory drink. I had stopped drinking in 2011 in preparation for Hugo's prosecution and vowed not to drink until after we got Hugo. But I didn't go.

I went straight home.

Nicole was waiting at the door, tears in her eyes. I wrapped her in a hug and didn't let go. She had carried so much of this weight with me—quietly, daily, without asking for anything in return. I often wondered if she thought I was crazy or if I was in over my head. Our little family had been in this fight just as much as I had.

The fight with Hugo wasn't mine alone. It belonged to all of us.

The kids came running in. "Daddy, you won, right?"

I nodded. "Yeah, Daddy won."

My daughter, Victoria, who was just two and a half years old, looked at me with that same fierce innocence she always had. She didn't understand that I was a prosecutor; she actually thought I had fought Hugo.

It didn't help that I trained like crazy in general and would spend countless hours punching a heavy bag in their presence. To her, Hugo was the man I'd been preparing to fight in a ring all these years. She asked me, "Did you get hurt, Daddy?"

I didn't know how to answer at first, because it hadn't been that kind of fight. And it wasn't that kind of hurt. But I was hurt and broken, just not on the outside. I said, "Daddy didn't get hurt, baby. As long as you love me, nothing hurts Daddy."

I went upstairs and showered. I was in a bit of shock. I threw on sweats and came back downstairs.

I walked into the toy room. Dominick was playing Mario Brothers. I picked up a controller and joined him. We played for a while. Later, I lay next to Nicole that night and said, "We got him. I can't believe it. We got him."

It was the first night of something new. Something free.

On Friday, February 13, 2015, I woke up early. For a second, I thought maybe it had all been a dream. I went downstairs, opened the front door, and picked up the paper.

The headline stopped me cold: "Sweet Relief." The photo on the cover of the *Citizens' Voice* was a picture of me holding Gerry Kerkowski's hand, walking with Salavantis and Sanguedolce.

I remembered my promise, "When this is over, they're going to take our picture." It was the image I had seen in my mind over all those years.

That picture hangs in my office to this day.

Hugo was convicted, but the case wasn't over yet.

On February 17, 2015, we began the final phase of the case. Our team enlisted additional prosecutors: Bill Finnegan, my friend and law partner, and Luke Moran, who helped our team with research for the penalty phase.

I delivered the opening statement in that phase. It wasn't easy for me, having come to know Hugo over the previous nine years, to now switch gears and ask for the jury to kill him.

Despite my familiarity with Hugo, I thought about the fact that he'd known his victims and never shown them mercy. So I stood and delivered the opening.

I reminded the jury that we had been on a journey through the world of Hugo Selenski. I told them that now we would be going on a journey through the life of Hugo Selenski and our own lives, that somehow our lives and Hugo's life had all crossed paths at that moment.

I told the jury that our lives are often a "series of decisions we make and paths we take," that we were there because of the decisions that Hugo had made. While pointing at Hugo, I argued that his life was hanging in the balance because of the path he'd chosen. He'd chosen money over life.

The aggravating circumstance the jury could consider in support of death was that Hugo and Weakley had tortured Michael. I reminded the jury first of the rolling pin. I said, "This isn't a murder weapon; it's a torture weapon."

I described how Michael had been taken downstairs and how his feet and hands had been bound. I noted that his eyes had been covered with duct tape—not so he couldn't see his attackers, as he knew who they were, but to disorient him, to cause fear and fright. He'd been beaten and strangled repeatedly. All while his girlfriend Tammy was restrained upstairs. I said, "That's terror torture, with a capital *T*."

Hugo's history of violent felonies was also an aggravating circumstance. I told the jury that Hugo was a convicted bank robber.

Finally, I was anticipating that Hugo's family, who had supported him throughout his trials, would testify on his behalf. I told the jury that their love and support, while commendable, made his crimes more confounding to me.

I reminded the jury not to be fooled by the fact that Hugo had a loving family. I made the point that he may have been among them as sheep, but he was a "wolf in sheep's clothing and that's the worst kind."

Sam did the closing for the death phase. He challenged the jurors to weigh the aggravating factors against any mitigation. A jury at that point isn't asked to weigh innocence or guilt—they are asked to determine if the state has proven the aggravating circumstances outweigh any mitigation evidence of the defendant. If the aggravating evidence outweighs the mitigation, then the jury is to impose death. If mitigation outweighs the aggravating evidence, the defendant receives a life sentence without the possibility of parole in Pennsylvania.

In the end, the jury elected to spare Hugo's life. He would die in the hands of the state but not *at* the hands of the state.

At one point as the jury read its verdict that would spare Hugo's life, I looked over at Hugo. I saw fear, then relief. It was the first time I had ever seen Hugo appear remotely afraid.

The trial was finally over. Hugo had been sentenced to two consecutive life sentences without the possibility of parole.

After the verdict and sentence, Hugo said to me, "No hard feelings, Ferentino."

I smiled and responded, "No hard feelings, Hugo."

Our team, along with Gerry and Lisa, accepted the jury's decision.

A few weeks later, a fruit basket arrived at my private office. There was a card attached. I opened it, and it read "thank you" on the front. Inside it read:

> Jarrett, All I have to say is "WOW" you did a fabulous job at the trial. I am so proud of you, and like you promised me and Mike you would never give up until the end.

Thank you for all of your hard work and dedication. Me, Mike and Michael were so lucky you have you on our side. I thank God for you. Gerry Kerkowski.

I smiled, and my eyes welled up. After winning a big case in private practice, you may receive a big check. After all these years, it meant more to me to know that Gerry Kerkowski was proud of me. That was all I needed.

I called my mom and read it to her. I said, "See, Mom, all your work wasn't in vain."

I told her I'd done it for her. She said she was proud, and not only for me. "You did it for your babies, too," she told me.

These cases aren't supposed to last nine years. No one designs their life around that kind of siege. But that's what it became—a long and brutal siege, a chess match against a mind that thrived on manipulation and malevolence.

That "game" changed people. It broke some, killed some. It scarred others.

It changed me too.

But it also proved something I needed to know about myself—that no matter how long the game, no matter how twisted the board, I'd stay standing until the end.

And that everything it cost was worth what it brought.

In the days and weeks following the trial, I would fall asleep if I sat down. I felt as if my body was healing and letting go of all of the darkness and angst that I'd been carrying for nine years. I was exhausted but relieved. There were also days when I couldn't believe it had happened and that it was over.

I remember sitting alone a lot, just feeling grateful and hoping I could somehow return to being the person I'd been before all this madness had begun. I realized there was no going back, but there was moving on.

So much couldn't be undone. Hurricane Hugo was real; it had destroyed almost everything in its path, but I'd mostly survived. The dead are still dead in his wake.

So many victims and so many lives destroyed. It has left me with some scars, I must admit.

I think about Hugo every day, probably more than anyone knows. How can a person be capable of such evil and still have glimpses of humanity? Was I just like him but with better control over the monster in me?

Through these crimes and killings, courthouse events and corruption, my psyche was tested.

Ever since the case, I've been more guarded with people. I find I don't like loud noises, bright lights, or strong smells. I have no idea what all of that is about. But in a world that leaves its victims bound and broken, I live free from my bonds and am healing from anything that Hugo broke or tried to break in me.

Nicole, Dominick, and Victoria shared me with Hugo for a long time. I could not have done what I did without their love, understanding, and support.

Hugo and Weakley remain incarcerated for life.

The skeletal remains of a fifth body found on Hugo's property remain unidentified despite law enforcement's best efforts.

In October 2019, Gerry Kerkowski passed away.

Detective Gary "Cap" Capitano retired in 2019. I would text him regularly, checking in and teasing him. On July 18, 2021, he passed away after a brief illness.

His wife, Angie, called and said, "Gary said if something ever happened to him that he wanted 'the kid' [me] to do his eulogy." I was honored and so proud to deliver his eulogy before his family, friends, and our entire team at the Luzerne County Courthouse.

I told funny stories about Cap, but I made it clear that I loved him. I thought to myself about the day that I jumped in his car after the first Hugo loss. We'd hardly known each other then, and here I was delivering his eulogy thirteen years later.

In February 2021, Stefanie Salavantis ran for judge and was elected. As a result, Sam Sanguedolce was appointed district attorney. He then ran and was elected district attorney in November 2021.

Many press outlets had been covering the trial, as I mentioned. Early in the trial, a member of the press approached me in a hallway. He introduced himself as Steph Watts, an investigative journalist from New York City.

He told me how he'd covered the biggest criminal trials in the country. I recognized him from some of the true crime television shows that I had seen.

He said, "I've never seen anything like that opening statement. You belong on television, and I am going to put you on."

I laughed and said, "Oh really? I bet you tell all the lawyers that."

I was standing with Cap, who rarely left my side during the trial. I introduced Steph to Cap and jokingly said, "Give him a television show; he's a character." Steph persisted and said he was serious. He asked if we could talk when all this was over. I assured him that I would be happy to.

We met several weeks later at my private office. Steph has become one of my closest friends, and as promised, he did put me on television, as a legal analyst.

LESSONS IN MOTIVATION: WHAT THE HUGO SELENSKI CASE TAUGHT ME ABOUT ENDURANCE, OBSESSION, AND LEGACY

Some cases change your career. A few change your life. And then there are the rare ones that redefine you—mind, body, and soul.

The Selenski case was that last one for me.

For nearly a decade, it wasn't just a case file. It became my internal compass. It tested my loyalty, pushed my resilience, and at times threatened to pull me under.

But it also taught me everything I know about staying the course when everything around you shifts.

These aren't just lessons from court transcripts or news headlines. These are lessons carved out in the quiet moments—the long runs with prison tapes in my ears, the hallway conversations with grieving families, the bedtime stories with my children interrupted by late-night strategy sessions.

For those of you navigating your own long game, be it personal or professional, here's what I've learned about when the spotlight fades and all that's left is grit.

Purpose Outlasts Politics

During the nine years as we prepared for trial, my team's leadership changed. Loyalties shifted. My welcome letter from the new district attorney was missing from the mailbox when others received theirs. But none of it mattered when I remembered the promise I had made to the families. When you're anchored in purpose, no title, administration, or election can take it away.

The takeaway: if your mission depends on who's in charge, it's not your mission. Build your identity around impact, not approval.

Obsession Isn't Dangerous—Unless It's Empty

I lived inside that case. I created a war room. I fell asleep on case files. Ran miles listening to Hugo's prison tapes. Some called it obsession. But obsession grounded in principle? That's fuel. That's how you win.

The takeaway: let people call you obsessed. Just make sure your obsession is with something that matters.

Loneliness Is the Entry Fee for Doing It Right

There were seasons when I stood alone—in courtrooms, in internal meetings, even in my own mind. You don't get to be the last man standing without spending time standing alone.

The takeaway: when no one claps, keep going. When they forget your name, keep working. Your mission's not about applause—it's about outcome.

Resilience Is a Decision, Not a Trait

I didn't wait for the District Attorney's Office to hand me an opportunity. I went to them. I didn't assume someone else would carry the case across the finish line. I made sure I did. I wasn't given this case because I was some great lawyer. I volunteered, knowing it could be what would make me great.

The takeaway: resilience isn't just getting back up; it's choosing to fight when no one's asking you to.

Your Legacy Lives in Private Moments

The courtroom win was public. But the legacy? That was the photo of me holding Gerry Kerkowski's hand after the verdict—the one that hangs in my office. Justice wasn't in the verdict. It was in what it gave back to the survivors of Hugo's many victims.

The takeaway: the world sees headlines; your soul remembers the quiet victories. Fight for the latter.

PRACTICAL STEPS FOR STAYING MOTIVATED IN YOUR LONGEST BATTLES

If you're in the thick of something hard—something long—these things might help you. They helped me stay locked in when everything said, *Let go.*

Anchor Your Mission in People, Not Positions

Your job may change. Your title may vanish. But people remain. I didn't fight for politics—I fought for Tammy, Michael, and their families.

Do this: write down the names of three people whose lives are impacted by your work. Look at that list when your motivation fades.

Make a Move After Every Rejection

No letter in the mailbox. New leadership. Team in limbo. I scheduled a meeting with the new DA, made my case for staying on, and created a new opportunity.

Do this: after a rejection, make a "next move" list. Then take one action before the week ends.

Systematize Your Passion

I didn't just "want" justice. I planned for it. Built routines. Created structure. Passion fades without a plan.

Do this: turn your goal into a weekly schedule. What must happen on Monday to get you closer by Friday?

Keep a Symbol That Grounds You

The photo of me holding Gerry's hand wasn't about the press; it was about a promise kept. When the noise gets loud, that image reminds me of what matters.

Do this: place one object—photo, quote, relic—where you work. Make it a totem of your purpose. You'll always be reminded of what you truly fight for.

Book 5

THE SPRING BREAK MURDER

South Carolina v. Raymond Moody

"I don't believe in closure. I believe in resolution."

—Dawn Drexel, Brittanee Drexel's mother

CHAPTER 1

SLOWING DOWN

ON THE EVENING OF MARCH 4, 2020, I was called to a shooting in Wilkes-Barre.

I arrived on Schuler Street and walked past the emergency service vehicles and onlookers, slipping under the crime scene tape. The police were gathered around a vehicle pulled to the side of the street.

Another shooting in the city, another young life lost, another perpetrator on the run.

The investigators briefed me. A man named Jeremy Gittens, age thirty-eight, had shot and killed Ryan McGovern, thirty-two, over an alleged short on a previous drug deal. Gittens had fled the scene.

My homicide cases—and the bodies—were piling up again but I was no longer a young prosecutor trying to prove himself. I had many additional responsibilities. I remember another Assistant District Attorney Shana Messinger on the scene. She was young and relatively new to the office I saw in her the excitement that I once had every time a murder came in.

That morning, I had prepped for a hearing in another homicide involving four juvenile defendants who'd conspired to rob and brutally murder one of their grandfathers.

The week before, I'd attended the arraignment of a young man named Zien Council, who'd senselessly executed and robbed a young woman named Brittney Reynolds. I had more homicide cases than any assistant district attorney in the office at the time, on top of dozens of cases on the regular trial list.

My private practice was also growing. I was scheduled to conduct labor negotiations for a school district client the next day.

But when a murder happens and the suspect is in the wind, we're at THREATCON Delta. Everything else stops.

I had always been willing to take on more, but I was stretched way too thin.

For the next few days, I worked out of the Wilkes-Barre City Police Department. The poorly lit rows of cubicles and white-boards felt familiar.

I loved days like this. I'd set up a makeshift war room with the detectives, monitor developments, and sit in on interviews.

Sometimes I met victims' families for the first time. Other times, I was back behind the two-way mirror while officers were questioning a suspect. The detectives and I would talk about old cases and current ones.

We'd joke, even in the gravity of the moment. It was part of the bond that comes with this work. I respected these detectives, and they respected me. We had history.

And I still loved that part of the job.

But the rest of life kept going. My responsibilities didn't vanish because of a murder. It had been five years since the Hugo Selenski case ended, and I was starting to wonder if it was time to step away from the District Attorney's Office. To devote more time to being a husband, father, and civil lawyer. I was starting to feel like I'd proven everything I needed to prove to myself as a prosecutor. I kept those thoughts to myself, but they were getting louder.

On March 5, 2020, officers apprehended Gittens in New York. Homicide charges were filed and pending. I was putting the finishing touches on the search warrants from my workspace at the police department. On television, President Donald Trump was in nearby Scranton, taping a Fox News town hall.

COVID-19 was beginning to take over the news cycle.

A member of the town hall audience asked the president what plans were being made at the federal level to handle the long-term disruption of the virus. President Trump said that the polling company Gallup had given him tremendous marks on his initial response.

He said he'd closed borders to countries with big outbreaks. At that point, there were 149 cases in the United States, compared with hundreds of thousands globally.

Less than two weeks later, the world shut down.

On March 17, 2020, the courthouse closed. The District Attorney's Office went remote. My private practice closed, Nicole's chiropractic clinic shut down, and my children's schools followed.

For the first time, like so many others, I slowed down.

I would wake up early and go for long runs outside. Nicole and the kids were home, and I'd return to find the house full of life. I'd work until noon in my home office, then stop.

Dave Pedri, now the Luzerne County manager, asked me to help build a Luzerne County COVID task force. I took charge of that and enjoyed conferring with Dave and our team as new challenges arose. We looked for ways to support the community during the shutdown.

I'd break for lunch with Nicole and the kids. In January 2019, we bought a new home, perched in the hills overlooking

Pittston, which gave everyone their own space—plus it had a spacious home office, a pool, a large yard, a pool table, and enough TVs and games to keep everyone occupied. But as in every good Italian house, the kitchen was our universe.

Our yard was full of flowers, trees, and shrubs. The kids spent hours outside. I taught Victoria to ride a bike. I even started painting in my home office. The kids and their cousins would request paintings, and I'd deliver.

Nicole and I cherished the tranquility of the lockdown. Up until then, we'd both been running ourselves ragged with work, never pausing.

Suddenly, the pause was here.

I spent my afternoons outside doing yardwork, listening to podcasts, and staying on call for clients and the District Attorney's Office. I would joke that I was practicing law in the dirt.

We had early dinners, movie nights, no practices, and no lessons. A break from chaos.

I could feel my brain healing from fifteen years of nonstop motion. I'd been buried in murder and mayhem, started a family, moved houses, and built a business. I'd never stopped long enough to look back.

But now, I did. I'm not one to dwell in the past, but the quiet pulled me into reflection.

I started to think that maybe it was time to move on from the murder-and-mayhem business. I began jotting down thoughts and memories. That became the beginning of this book.

CHAPTER 2

A NEW JOURNEY

STEPH WATTS, THE INVESTIGATIVE JOURNALIST I'd met during the Selenski trial, had become one of my closest friends. He was always on the move, connected to almost every major case in the country.

He'd worked with Nancy Grace and Greta Van Susteren. He covered the big-name cases: Casey Anthony, Natalee Holloway, Bill Cosby, and others.

Steph was living alone in New York during COVID. I checked in with him regularly. We'd talk as I worked in the yard, swapping thoughts on big cases. Once, he called Jeffrey Dahmer's lawyer on the line. Another time, it was a Cosby victim.

One day in June 2020, he called and mentioned Brittanee Drexel, a seventeen-year-old from Chili, New York, who'd vanished in Myrtle Beach, South Carolina, during a 2009 spring break trip. He worked her case for the *Crime Watch Daily* TV series and has known her mother, Dawn Drexel, since 2011.

I'd certainly heard of the Brittanee Drexel case. It felt like the kind of story every parent shares before their child leaves for spring break. I had seen Dawn Drexel on the national news, *Dr. Phil*, and *Nancy Grace*.

Steph said he had been talking with Dawn. She was tired, frustrated. Investigators had been giving her the runaround for over a decade. A new FBI team was taking over the case, but her trust had been shattered.

She wanted a lawyer by her side. Someone to help her keep the pressure on and to translate what was really happening.

Without asking me, Steph had told her that I was the guy. That's Steph.

He said she wanted to talk to me. Maybe I could help.

I hesitated. My mind had been healing. I knew that life would eventually roar back, and I'd promised myself I wouldn't return to the same pace. I was seriously thinking at that point of walking away from the District Attorney's Office.

I asked Steph, "What could I do for her? I don't even have a license in South Carolina." I complained that the last thing I needed was another murder case, let alone a cold one hundreds of miles away.

He said, "You can listen. Just take one call."

As a lawyer, I know how that goes. One call, one letter—never just one. But I agreed to speak with Dawn.

As the great Al Pacino said, playing Michael Corleone in *The Godfather Part III*, "Just when I thought I was out, they pull me back in!"

Before speaking with Dawn, I started looking deeper into Brittanee's case.

Brittanee Drexel was born on October 7, 1991, in Rochester, New York, to John Kahyaoglu and Dawn Wagner. Dawn then married Chad Drexel, and he adopted Brittanee. The family resided in the suburb of Chili after Chad's military service concluded.

Brittanee was her family's world. She was beautiful, funny, and outgoing. An active high school junior and soccer player, Brittanee had planned to pursue nursing, cosmetology, or even modeling.

In April 2009, Brittanee asked to go to Myrtle Beach, South Carolina, for spring break with friends. Dawn refused, due to a lack of adult supervision and her unfamiliarity with the other teens. Brittanee relented and said she would spend the break at a friend's lake house. Dawn was OK with that compromise.

Despite this, Brittanee actually left for Myrtle Beach on April 22, 2009, saying she was going to her friend's lake house for the week instead.

While in Myrtle Beach, she and her friends stayed at the Bar Harbor hotel. On April 25, at around 8 p.m., she left the hotel on foot to visit friends at the nearby Bluewater Resort, about one and a half miles away.

Security cameras captured her arrival there, wearing a black-and-white tank top, shorts, and flip-flops, and carrying a beige purse.

At approximately 8:45 p.m., she left that resort. This was the last confirmed sighting of Brittanee. She texted her boyfriend, John Grieco (who remained in New York due to work), to say she was heading back to the Bar Harbor hotel.

Her messages abruptly stopped around 9:15 p.m., after which Grieco attempted to contact friends back home in Myrtle Beach, then called Dawn to report that Brittanee was in Myrtle Beach and now missing.

CHAPTER 3

VANISHED

DAWN DREXEL WAS SHOCKED TO learn that Brittanee was in Myrtle Beach. Multiple calls and texts to Brittanee's phone went unanswered. Dawn was panicking. She then reached out to Rochester police and they asked to coordinate with South Carolina authorities.

Dawn called John Haan, a trusted friend who lived in North Carolina. She asked him to get to Myrtle Beach. After hours had passed, Dawn headed to Myrtle Beach and met with investigators.

Myrtle Beach police began actively searching the next morning, retrieving security footage from the Bluewater Resort to verify Brittanee's last known location.

They identified her last known contact as being with a man named Peter Brozowitz—a nightclub promoter from Rochester who was vacationing in Myrtle Beach. The police interviewed him and the others he was vacationing with, ruling no one in or out at that stage.

Police combed through Brittanee's hotel room and recovered all her belongings that remained, but her purse and cell phone were missing. They interviewed the friends she had traveled there with who had no information regarding Brittanee's whereabouts.

Investigators tracked her phone's last network pings to an area approximately fifty miles south of Myrtle Beach, near the Georgetown–Charleston County line.

The phone had stopped sending signals early on April 26. This led to an eleven-day search of the surrounding areas, including swamps along US Route 17. Brittanee's disappearance became national news.

Long after Brittanee Drexel vanished into the humid South Carolina night in April 2009, and long after the search dogs searched in the brush near the Santee River, the case remained open but cold.

Dawn never stopped fighting, never stopped asking questions. But the answers were elusive. She organized searches with volunteers for years. They would canvas neighborhoods and hand out flyers with Brittanee's picture. Dawn raised money and purchased billboards showing Brittanee's picture. She refused to stop searching or to just go away. Everyone in Myrtle Beach knew about the Brittanee Drexel case and Dawn refused to let them forget it. The years passed with no answers.

Then, in 2016, seven years after Brittanee had disappeared, hope came roaring back in the most shocking of ways. The FBI took over the investigation.

FBI agents announced that they'd had a breakthrough, and they offered a twenty-five-thousand-dollar reward for anyone with information. The "breakthrough" was made clearer in a court appearance a few weeks later.

An informant—an inmate named Taquan Brown—claimed he had witnessed the final moments of Brittanee's life inside a notorious "stash house," a place used to store drugs, guns, money, and other contraband for gangs, in the rural town of McClellanville, South Carolina.

He said he'd seen her being sexually assaulted by several men. He said she'd tried to run. One of them had pistol-whipped her. And then, he said, she'd been murdered, her body wrapped in a rug and dumped into an alligator-infested swamp.

The name Brown gave to federal agents was chillingly specific: Timothy Da'Shaun Taylor.

It was as if the storm that had been hovering above the Drexel family for years suddenly shifted, now unleashing its fury on a single person.

Taylor had been just sixteen years old when Brittanee went missing. He hadn't been some unknown drifter or hardened criminal. He'd been a local kid, living with his family in a modest South Carolina home.

He'd lost part of his left arm in a childhood accident. He wore a prosthetic. He played sports. He had his troubles, sure. He'd been involved in a McDonald's robbery as a teen. But he had served his time. He was trying to rebuild.

That didn't matter.

The FBI's new theory painted Taylor and members of his family as part of a brutal sex-trafficking ring. They claimed he'd helped lure Brittanee from Myrtle Beach to McClellanville, where she'd been raped and then murdered to silence her. Another unnamed inmate confirmed it.

Taylor's name and these developments made national headlines.

Dawn's nightmare grew darker, and her worst fears were realized. Dawn endured hearing that Brittanee had been kidnapped, gang-raped, pistol-whipped, shot, wrapped in a rug, and fed to alligators.

The words burned into the public's imagination.

The Taylor family was stunned. Their son, they insisted, was innocent. He had been in school. There was no physical evidence, no DNA, no fingerprints, no surveillance footage. Just the word of two inmates desperate for leniency.

Still, the FBI pressed on.

They couldn't charge Taylor with Brittanee's murder. There was no body, no hard proof. So they reached back in time. They filed federal charges against him for the 2011 McDonald's robbery he had already pleaded guilty to in state court, a maneuver that many saw as a pressure tactic. Taylor had already served time. Now he was facing a second punishment for the same crime.

And behind the scenes, agents told his lawyer that unless Taylor gave them more on Brittanee, they'd pursue the maximum sentence.

By 2019, however, the prison informant's story, once so confidently delivered, had begun to unravel. The "truth" was crumbling. And so was the FBI's theory.

For years since the initial announcement, Taylor had been living in a kind of purgatory—never convicted but never truly free. He and his family had been threatened, harassed, and shunned. Reporters had knocked on their doors.

Rumors chased them through the streets of Charleston and Goose Creek. Taylor lost jobs. He lost peace. His name remained entangled in Brittanee's.

No arrest was made. And Brittanee remained missing. Years began to tick by again.

CHAPTER 4

DARKEST BEFORE DAWN

IN JUNE 2020, I SPOKE with Dawn for the first time. I went in with a plan to just listen and be supportive. To not commit to getting involved.

I spoke with so many victims over the course of my career. She echoed the familiar refrain—that the system was broken, corrupt, and that it had failed her. I could hear the anger in her voice, the grief layered beneath it.

Dawn had lived this story for more than a decade. Dawn had fought for Brittanee and struggled to keep working and raise her family. Her world had fallen apart. She was broke, and she was broken. But she wasn't hopeless.

Dawn was sharp. Feisty and direct. She didn't sugarcoat anything and knew when to speak plainly, even vulgarly, when needed. She told me about Brittanee. How young Dawn had been when she had her with her then boyfriend, John Kahyaoglu.

How she'd later married Chad Drexel, who'd adopted Brittanee, and how they'd had two more children together, Myrissa and Camdyn.

She described Brittanee with fierce love, saying she was beautiful. Kind. Tough. An athlete. A fighter.

She told me little tidbits of information about Brittanee: how she loved fashion, loved frogs, and was feared on the soccer field.

She told me that Brittanee had an eye condition and that she had to wear a certain kind of contact lens.

She shared how things had begun to unravel during and after Dawn's separation from Chad, how Brittanee had started to act out. She was partying, depressed, and running with a new crowd prior to her disappearance. It was clear that Dawn adored her family. And it was even clearer that she would never stop fighting for her daughter.

Dawn told me that the FBI had taken over Brittanee's case. She relived the Taylor story with me. I could appreciate her frustration and distrust of investigators after years had passed since their "breakthrough" press conference. She needed my help now because a new team of agents had been assigned. She'd been speaking with one of them regularly, Agent Michael Connolly.

Dawn was jaded and suspicious of law enforcement. She was hearing whispers of corruption and all kinds of claims.

She connected me with agents Mike Connolly, James Cavanaugh, and Caleb Messer. I reached out to Agent Connolly. He was approachable, professional, and reassuring. He said that the FBI was planning to, at some point, brief Dawn, along with members of the many departments and prosecutors who'd been working on the case.

Dawn asked if I could attend the meeting, even if just remotely. "If you're there with me," she said, "they won't play games. They'll know we aren't going away."

So much for my plan not to get too involved. I listened to her voice, to the urgency behind her words. "I need you to make sure they're not full of shit," she said, in the most Dawn way possible. I agreed to help however I could. I would attend the meeting.

Actually, I don't even remember if Dawn actually asked me to help or if I'd been willing. Dawn and I just started talking, and we clicked. It was clear I was on board. After all, I promised my mother I would help mothers who needed me. I took Dawn's case for no fee. This wasn't about money; it was about repaying a debt to my own mother.

I joined the meeting remotely. The FBI investigative team, the US Attorney's Office, Myrtle Beach Police, state prosecutors, and local departments were all represented. I listened closely. The agents laid out a new strategy. They were experienced. Passionate. Focused.

Afterward, Dawn called me. "What do you think?" she asked.

I assured Dawn that everything I'd been hearing seemed positive and that this new group of agents was clearly motivated. That they had direction. That their behavior wasn't performative. They hadn't just held the meeting to check a box or appease her. They meant what they'd said.

Agent Connolly welcomed me as Dawn's counsel. We would speak occasionally as the case developed. I'd check in to ask questions or hear updates. Agent Connolly is an incredible investigator and is relentless. He was also compassionate and patient with Dawn. He was committed to helping her and I recognized that immediately. I appreciate that kind of intensity and obsession. I had lived it during the Hugo Selenski case for almost a decade. I knew that's what it would take to find actual answers and move Brittanee's case.

Dawn and Steph often would call me together. She would brief me on her calls with the investigators. Ask me what I thought. Sometimes she was up. Other times, she was deep in the darkness. I could usually tell from the tone—some calls started with a long sigh. Those were the tough days.

We remained in contact with one another, and I would review whatever information I could get my hands on in Brittanee's case. Agent Connolly provided us with regular updates over the next year and a half.

CHAPTER 5

DIGGING DEEPER

IN MARCH 2022, I REMOTELY attended another high-level meeting with the investigative team; Dawn was present as well. Agent Connolly laid out the FBI agents' findings. He and his team had spent months narrowing Brittanee's movements. They'd tracked her along Ocean Boulevard, between the Bar Harbor hotel and Bluewater Resort.

They'd conducted an extensive video canvas, enhancing old footage, reviewing lab reports, analyzing files from multiple agencies in Myrtle Beach, Georgetown, and Rochester, and from the South Carolina Law Enforcement Division.

They'd reviewed tips, cross-checked hotel records, consulted a cell phone expert, and sequenced traffic with license plate readers. They'd traced Brittanee's cell phone. Her texts with her boyfriend back in Rochester had suddenly stopped. The crucial window: 8:59 to 9:05 p.m.

They'd mapped her walking path. She never made it past Eleventh Avenue. Around 9:05 p.m., her phone had begun moving as if it were in a vehicle, heading away from Myrtle Beach.

It later pinged near North Santee and the Santee River. From 10:16 p.m. to nearly midnight, the phone had remained in that area until it went silent, either smashed or submerged.

The mood in the meeting shifted.

The agents no longer spoke in broad terms but about actual individuals. Though they didn't reveal names, they described "Person A" and "Person B." I know what that means. I know that means answers and possibly more.

These individuals lived within twenty miles of where Brittanee's phone had last pinged. They had connections to a vehicle caught on video. And they weren't strangers to this kind of violence.

The agents had reason to believe that Person A and Person B were connected to Brittanee's disappearance. They'd been reviewing and enhancing hours and hours of video footage; they were looking for a vehicle with a connection to Person A and Person B in the videos.

At last, they had found a match on the video. They had corroborated the evidence. The agents were going to confront the individuals soon.

The investigators told us that things were moving. And fast. They committed to keeping us updated on a weekly basis as well.

Dawn called me immediately after the meeting. The tone of her voice was different. Hopeful, finally. We both believed that the end was near. After thirteen years, the team was closing in.

Over the next several weeks, Dawn and I spoke nearly every day. She stayed in touch with the agents. She pushed them. Asked for updates. Rehashed conversations.

She had other people in her corner—family, friends, supporters. I knew she called them, too. But my role was to be steady. To absorb her panic when it surfaced. To manage and predict where we were headed.

Then one day, Dawn called and said that Person A had a name: Raymond Moody.

I knew the name. Raymond Moody had been a suspect early on in Brittanee's disappearance. Investigators at one point had searched a motel room he had stayed in. A reporter had even confronted him regarding Brittanee. He was on my list of Brittanee suspects that hadn't been crossed out. I didn't have access to the case file and had to rely on what I could get my hands on from Dawn and conversations with Agent Connolly. I was always suspicious of Moody but for some reason the trail to him ran cold. That was about to change.

Raymond Moody had been hiding in plain sight. A convicted sex offender with a history soaked in violence, he'd spent twenty-one years in prison for abducting and raping a nine-year-old girl in California back in 1983. There had been whispers—more victims, more horror, shallow graves—but charges had never come. Just gaps.

He'd been a person of interest in Brittanee's case for years, the kind of man whose name always lingered in the margins of a missing girl's file. Because the day after Brittanee vanished, Moody had been pulled over near Myrtle Beach. Just a traffic stop. But the timing screamed. I used to think to myself, *Here's this great white shark named Raymond Moody in the water near Brittanee.*

Then Moody's former cellmate and ex-boyfriend, Ernie Merchant, had gone to the authorities around the time Brittanee went missing to tell them that Raymond Moody had scratches on his face and had taken a shovel from his house. Moody and Ernie had recently separated, and Moody was acting strange around the time Brittanee disappeared. He had also begun dating a woman named Angel Vause.

Years passed and any suspicion upon Moody waned as the investigation crept along.

Angel Vause also went to the police in April 2011. She claimed that when he'd been her boyfriend, Moody had had "nightmarish fantasies of torture and death," as she put it. She said he was obsessed with violent pornography and had been aroused by reenacting his past sexual crimes using Vause as a substitute for the victims.

Vause claimed that Moody would threaten her, saying that if she were ever to leave him, he'd abduct another girl to fulfill his sadistic desires.

Vause even told police she was worried that Moody might have kidnapped and killed Brittanee but couldn't say for sure. Her story kept changing. Vause later told a story about how when Moody was in a McDonald's, he saw a billboard with Brittanee's picture on it. He said to Vause, "I wish she [Dawn] would just go the fuck away already."

In 2022, when the agents finally confronted Moody with their video footage of a vehicle tied to him and Vause and all the evidence that they'd compiled to date, he confessed that he and Vause had together picked up Brittanee as she was walking down the street, asking if she wanted to party and smoke marijuana.

The three of them together had ended up at a campsite in Georgetown County, where Moody had kidnapped, raped, and killed Brittanee.

Vause and Moody claimed to investigators that Vause had gone to pick up keys during the time of the actual murder itself.

Moody's confession was important, but investigators believed he was insulating Vause. They took Moody into custody on lesser charges to hold him as they then began a search for Brittanee's body.

The investigators pressed Moody for the location of Brittanee's body. He traveled with them to the wooded area in

Georgetown, where he claimed to have buried her. They were going to start digging.

Investigators prepared to recover the truth.

Moody led them into the brush off Pickerel Road, his confession already echoing behind him: “She’s buried about four feet down.” Dawn and I were aware of the search and dig. We spoke every day at this point, monitoring the progress and news from investigators.

The first crews—Georgetown County sheriffs and the FBI—descended on private land near Pickerel Road, a dozen miles from the Myrtle Beach boardwalk. They chopped saplings. They cut paths. They rolled back the earth. For days. They worked methodically, grid by grid. They scanned one patch of dirt for signs of disturbance. No flags, no body bags—just hope dressed in gloves.

On day two, they found a clue: a single human bone. Gray, angular, dull in the Carolina sun. They dug deeper and kept mapping.

And they found more: fragments of bone, geological anomalies in the soil layers. They dug into the night. Seventeen hours straight. Dirt falling through fingers. Dust coating their sleeves.

Amid the residue, they uncovered what remained of what had once been a life: long, straight strands of hair draped over a fractured skull. A single blue contact lens still nestled in the socket—an artifact of Brittanee’s childhood eye condition.

A silver nose ring, tarnished by years underground. No clothing. No soft tissue. Nothing beyond recognizable artifacts and a skeleton.

Rooted bones. Synthetic plastic. A lens whose hue matched the color of Brittanee’s eyes in the faded Missing Person posters from 2009.

At last, investigators had a body. Bones don't tell everything—the forensic team could not see any strangulation marks due to decay, for instance. The team believed they found Brittanee but had to confirm her identity.

Within forty-eight hours, specialists cross-referenced dental records and DNA. Confirmation came. The bones were hers. Brittanee Drexel was found.

CHAPTER 6

FOUND

OVER THOSE DAYS WHILE THE team was still excavating, I kept checking in with Dawn, reassuring her to be patient and waiting for the call.

Then it came.

Dawn was crying as she said, "Jarrett, they found her."

Everything accelerated from there. I was in contact with the prosecutors and investigators. Moody would be charged in the coming days with Brittanee's kidnapping, rape, and murder. There was going to be a press conference, and they wanted Dawn to be a part of it.

Dawn and I spoke after we heard the plan. She asked me to travel to Myrtle Beach to be there with her.

We spoke with Agent Connolly. I cleared my calendar, canceled my upcoming appointments, and booked a flight to Myrtle Beach.

Word spread quickly—nationally and internationally. Reporters started circling. I turned to Steph and said he was now our media liaison for the legal team, officially for one dollar.

We weren't interested in the chaos of comments or playing media games. Steph, Dawn, and I agreed we'd work with a single national outlet. Not for money—just to make sure Brittanee's and

Dawn's stories would be told the right way. Intimate. Focused. Personal.

Steph reached out to ABC. Producers were interested. They committed to embedding a team in Myrtle Beach and planned interviews for *Good Morning America* and *20/20* following Moody's arrest. It felt right—and later would prove to be.

On May 15, 2022, I flew into Myrtle Beach and met Steph at the airport. We headed to the hotel where Dawn, her family, and a large contingent of supporters were staying. Outside, I met Dawn in person for the first time. We hugged, and she cried. I got emotional, too.

It's funny how these days, you can get to know someone from video calls, texts, and phone conversations. So when you finally meet, the connection is real, like that between old friends.

She looked strong and healthy. Her husband, Dave Conley, stood by her side. A true gentleman.

A circle of supporters surrounded her: her parents, volunteers, private investigators, and searchers who had walked this journey with her. I referred to them as "Dawn's army."

She took me around and introduced me to everyone, simply saying, "This is Jarrett." Everyone welcomed me, and it was clear they all had been briefed on who I was and what my role was.

I met Dawn's son, Camdyn Drexel. He had been just a little boy when his big sister Brittanee vanished. He was in college now and taking in everything that was happening.

But the tone of this trip surprised me. It wasn't heavy. It felt… bittersweet.

Brittanee's family hadn't been under any delusions. They had already accepted Brittanee's fate. The torture wasn't only in her death but in not knowing the details. Now they had answers. I couldn't help but smile as I met everyone.

I had arranged for a conference room at the hotel and sat down in it with Dawn and Steph. I had drafted a statement for Dawn to read at the press conference. We reviewed it together and made a few small edits.

I then met in the conference room with the ABC *20/20* crew: producer Denise Martinez-Ramundo and her team. They were professional and respectful. I let them know we wouldn't be camera-shy but that respect was nonnegotiable.

That evening, Dawn insisted that Steph and I go with her to a cookout hosted by her friends in the village of Murrells Inlet. They had opened their home to her during her search. It was a forty-five-minute drive out there.

Dave drove. Dawn rode up front. Steph and I sat in the back.

Dawn said, "Jarrett, I have to play this song for you. I've been listening to it while we were waiting for news from the search."

She played "Rescue" by Lauren Daigle.

As the song began to play, Dawn lit a cigarette and sat back with the window cracked open. Her big sunglasses on. Hair whipping in the wind.

I stared at her for a moment, thinking about all she had endured to get to this day. And here I was—six hundred miles from home, wrapped up in another murder case. Far from my own family, riding with people who had been strangers not long ago.

I listened closely. Every lyric hit like a wave. It was a love song between the singer and a lost love that sounded as if it had been written about Dawn and her search for Brittanee. A cry from Brittanee. A vow from Dawn.

Dawn had never stopped marching. Never stopped fighting.

A mother with few resources, from hundreds of miles away, had built an army. She'd brought her own investigators, journalists, volunteers, rescue teams, and search dogs.

Dawn had even brought her personal prosecutor to Brittanee's case, and it was me.

I was honored to be in her ranks. I was a little anxious, as I was a stranger in this town. I had no prosecutorial authority in the state; I wasn't licensed to practice law there. None of that mattered. I was there to be by Dawn's side. I wasn't going to take any bullshit, and Dawn was going to be heard.

We spent that evening surrounded by those who had stood by Dawn during those initial years of searches and awareness marches. We talked about life, not death. That felt right.

The next morning, May 16, I woke up early. I needed to run—my ritual before any big case. This time, I ran for eight miles on the beach. It cleared my head.

By the time I returned, reporters had already gathered outside the hotel. The parking lot was buzzing. I slipped into the hotel lobby and told our team I'd be down in thirty minutes.

When I came back, the lobby was packed.

A convoy of a dozen police cruisers had arrived to escort us to the investigator meeting and the press conference. ABC's crew followed us with cameras. Dawn, Camdyn, Steph, and I shared a car.

At one point, I looked at Dawn and said, "We wouldn't be here if it weren't for you. You never gave up."

She sipped her coffee, staring out the window, and replied with a quiet confidence and satisfaction, "She's my daughter."

Chad Drexel, Brittanee's adopted father, was there with his family, too.

We first traveled to the Georgetown County Sheriff's Department; Georgetown County Sheriff Carter Weaver and County Solicitor Jimmy Richardson greeted us. Dawn already knew many of them. I met them, along with the lead FBI agents,

Connolly and Cavanaugh, and Hank Carrison from the sheriff's department, in person for the first time.

They were always very cordial and respectful to me, even though I was an outsider. They were aware of my background and that I wasn't some ambulance-chasing lawyer.

Sheriff Weaver and Solicitor Richardson brought Dawn and me into a private meeting. They walked us through the charges against Moody and plans for the press conference. They told Dawn that she and her whole team could stand beside them.

Dawn listened, calm and steady.

She looked at me and said, "Do you have any questions for them?"

I did. I asked a few questions. The sheriff and solicitor were respectful and serious. No fluff. They were ready to prosecute Moody for Brittanee's murder and fight for Dawn, too.

When the public press conference took place later that day, I stood off to the left of the podium, watching Dawn, a mother who had borne the weight of thirteen years with more strength than any of us could imagine.

When she began speaking, she read the statement that we crafted. There wasn't fear or fragility in her voice. It was steel. She carried Brittanee with every word, every pause, every breath.

After thanking the various organizations for their efforts in finding Brittanee's remains, she read the words we'd written: "Today marks the beginning of a new chapter. The search for Brittanee is now a pursuit of Brittanee's justice."

Talk about power.

You could hear the collective exhalation in that room.

She didn't break. She didn't falter. She stood tall and unbowed, steely-eyed.

I kept thinking of how far she'd come—from frantic calls in 2009 to uprooting her whole life to Myrtle Beach to search, to enduring misinformation and false leads, to this. Dawn carried hope in her bones as much as grief. She carried resolve like armor.

Every time she said Brittanee's name, that name came alive. We were standing with a warrior, someone who had clawed back truth from the earth, unearthing a stolen life, excavation by excavation, word by fearless word.

When it ended, there was no applause. There didn't need to be. Dawn Drexel had already given us something more powerful: evidence of a mother's courage.

Everyone witnessed what it means to never surrender to despair, to fight until every shadow is lit by clarity.

CHAPTER 7

BURIAL GROUND AND ASHES

WE TRAVELED FROM THE PRESS conference in the same convoy of vehicles to where the investigators had found Brittanee's body. The drive took us deep into the woods, across a large parcel of private property. A new owner had purchased the land and had graciously welcomed the team out to the site.

You could still see signs of disturbed ground and evidence of the heavy equipment used during the excavation. Tracks marked the earth. We got out of the car, and Sheriff Weaver and Hank Garrison pointed out the exact location where Brittanee's remains had been found.

About thirty of us were standing there. I stayed close to Dawn, her family, Steph, and her supporters. The investigators stood nearby.

While we were there, Camdyn knelt in the dirt and drew a heart.

One of Dawn's cousins asked us to gather in prayer. We circled together. He led us in a short, heartfelt prayer.

Afterward, we returned to the hotel. Dawn and I cleaned up, then sat for our interview with *Good Morning America*, set to air the next morning.

Dawn was graceful and calm. I sat beside her, offering a few thoughts and expectations for the prosecution's case against Moody.

It had been a long day. We went to dinner. During the meal, our team received a call from a producer of *Crime Stories with Nancy Grace*. The producer asked Dawn to join the show the following morning. Nancy Grace had previously covered Brittanee's case, and Dawn was grateful. She agreed to appear and asked me to join. I agreed.

Later that evening, we visited the Tree of Life in Myrtle Beach, a memorial planted in Brittanee's honor. The tree stood at Grand Park at the Market Common. It had been planted ten years earlier, in 2012. Beneath it sat a headstone and a plaque with Brittanee's name and photo, and the tree was adorned with pictures and flowers that visitors had left. Dawn, Camdyn, and Dawn's parents stood quietly near the tree. Some cousins and friends joined as well. Steph and I stood with them.

In past conversations, Dawn had told me that Brittanee had loved frogs. I'd even seen a photo of her holding one. As we stood near the tree, a frog hopped down the pavement and settled close by. I pointed it out to Dawn, who immediately said, "It's a sign." Brittanee was with us.

We returned to the hotel that night. Dawn's family and friends, Steph, and some of the ABC crew gathered around the lobby and hotel pool. Some people had drinks. I lit a cigar.

We sat outside for several hours. It wasn't a sad night; we reflected on the day's events and laughed a little.

Around 11 p.m., I walked through the lobby. The news was on the TV. It felt surreal, being six hundred miles from home and watching this unfold on national television.

The next morning, May 17, 2022, I said goodbye to Dawn, Steph, and the rest of our growing team. We knew we'd be back together soon.

I got a ride to the airport and joined Nancy Grace's show. It was audio only, so I participated while walking through the airport using my AirPods. I was happy to have the chance to thank Nancy for shedding light on and supporting Dawn in Brittanee's case for many years.

Dawn was planning a celebration of life for Brittanee in Rochester that June. She'd never had the chance to hold a funeral for Brittanee. Her family and friends had never gotten to mourn Brittanee together. So Dawn was planning something beautiful.

I assured her that Nicole and I would be there.

The next month, Nicole and I drove out to Rochester for the celebration of life. Dawn greeted us at our hotel. She and Nicole were happy to finally meet in person.

I could tell that Dawn was nervous and had something to say. She reached into a bag she was holding and said, "I want you to have something." She handed me a box. I opened it. Inside was a locket with Brittanee's picture.

On the back, it read, "Forever in my heart." Dawn said the locket had some of Brittanee's ashes. "I want you to have it to remember Brittanee and us always," she told me.

I was deeply moved. I gave Dawn a hug and said thank you.

That evening, we had dinner with Dawn's army.

On June 11, 2022, Brittanee's celebration of life was held at the Father's House Church on Paul Road in Rochester. Hundreds of family and friends stood to share memories of Brittanee.

Myrissa Drexel, Brittanee's younger sister, spoke about how Brittanee had been her protector. She asked everyone to remember Brittanee for who she was, not just by how her story had ended.

Chad Drexel and his family were present, too. We shook hands and talked briefly.

Dawn introduced me to Brittanee's father, John Kahyaoglu.

During the ceremony, Dawn gifted additional lockets to the FBI agents. They were visibly emotional. I could tell they were honored. It was a reminder that there are still good, tough people doing hard work in this world.

I was proud to be there and to celebrate Brittanee's life alongside Dawn and her family.

A week later, on June 17, 2022, I traveled to New York City to film an interview for *20/20*. Dawn and her family were already in town.

Since becoming involved in the case, I'd learned that during Moody's previous twenty-year prison stint in California, he'd had a romantic partner named Ernie Merchant. Steph had been in touch with Ernie, who had moved to Myrtle Beach with Moody after their release.

Their relationship had ended just prior to the murder and after Moody met Vause. Ernie, once incarcerated for drug charges, had turned his life around. He'd cleaned up and opened a salon, and he was living honestly. Ernie was in New York to film with the *20/20* crew as well.

I was planning to meet Ernie and his husband, Stephen, along with the *20/20* team for dinner. I was curious about Ernie's story but cautious, too.

Then Steph called—he was running late. He told me that Ernie and Stephen were at the hotel bar and to go meet them.

I hesitated for a second. I thought, *Now I am going by myself to meet the killer's former cellmate and ex-boyfriend.* Yet another interesting twist in this wild ride.

Ernie and Stephen were both warm and welcoming. We chatted until Steph arrived, then we all headed to Tavern on the Green.

Ernie was open about his journey. He had been incarcerated in California following his arrest on drug charges. He told me about his life behind bars with Raymond Moody. He said they'd gone to South Carolina after leaving prison to build a new life. Things had fallen apart as Moody came off parole. Ernie had since built a new, successful, happy, and honest life. I enjoyed getting to know both him and Stephen.

Ernie even became a friend to Dawn. Ernie and Dawn had both been victimized by Raymond Moody, and they both wanted justice to find them. Their friendship grew from there.

The next morning, I ran through Central Park before the *20/20* interview. Then Steph, Ernie, Stephen, and I met up with the *20/20* crew at a studio on West 39th Street. I filmed my interview segment for *20/20*. I have come to enjoy doing television and media work. I love telling the stories of victims and cases in the courtroom and feel a similar pride in doing the same in the press. I left New York and headed home knowing Moody's plea and sentencing would be coming within the next several months.

That summer, I kept checking in with Dawn. We were waiting for a guilty plea and a sentencing date for Moody. I kept reviewing the case files, wondering if anything would ever come of Moody's girlfriend, Angel Vause, and her role.

The court date was set: October 19, 2022, at the Georgetown County Courthouse. Raymond Moody had been formally charged with Brittanee's kidnapping, rape, and murder. He would appear in court and plead guilty and would then likely be sentenced to life in prison.

On October 14, the *20/20* episode aired on ABC. It was titled "The Darkest Night," drawn from the Lauren Daigle song. Steph brought the song to *20/20*, and it was featured in the episode.

On October 18, I flew back to Myrtle Beach for court.

Steph picked me up at the airport. He told me that Ernie and Stephen wanted us to visit them on Pawleys Island, a coastal town about forty minutes south of Myrtle Beach. We went, and Ernie insisted on cutting my hair. I let him. He did a great job.

Later, Steph and I traveled to the Georgetown County Courthouse to meet up with the *20/20* team. They were filming another episode. We met with court personnel and members of the press to plan for the media onslaught that was expected the following day.

The courthouse was majestic. I stood there, trying to imagine how wild things would get there the next day.

After the meeting, we went to the house where Dawn was staying. Her army was there. We talked through the plans for the next morning.

That night, we had a great dinner with the *20/20* crew, Dawn's family, Ernie, and Stephen. People in the restaurant stared. The locals clearly had watched the *20/20* episode. They knew who we were. They knew why we were in town.

CHAPTER 8

JUDGMENT DAY

THE NEXT DAY, OCTOBER 19, I woke early and went for a run. It was still dark. Then I drove to the house where Dawn was staying. It was full of friends and family. The cameras were rolling as I pulled up and entered the house. This all plays out on *20/20*'s second episode featuring Brittanee's case.

John Kahyaoglu and some of Brittanee's childhood friends had made the trip, too.

I sat with Dawn to review her victim impact statement. We made some final edits. I told her and John to stay close.

Soon, we lined up in another convoy of vehicles and drove to the courthouse. I rode with Steph, Dawn, and John.

When we arrived, the crowd was overwhelming. Cameras, reporters, people everywhere.

I spotted a pastor as well as Timothy Da'Shaun Taylor and his family talking with the press.

We were led inside by a security detail of police and deputy sheriffs. They took us into an empty courtroom and briefed us on what to expect. We spoke with solicitor Jimmy Richardson and Sheriff Carter Weaver. They briefed us on what was going to happen in court and we reviewed Dawn's statement. Jimmy

Richardson told us that Keith Morrison from *Dateline* was in the courtroom and Moody had agreed to be interviewed by him.

Then we were called into the courtroom.

I sat with Dawn, John, and Steph. The left side of the room was packed with Dawn's family and friends. Cameras lined the jury box. This was a new experience for me. In Pennsylvania, we aren't allowed to have cameras in courtrooms.

I spotted familiar faces in the press, Keith Morrison's among them.

We waited, and then a door to the right opened. Deputies led Raymond Moody into the courtroom.

Dawn tensed. She had waited thirteen years for this moment.

I was honored to be by her side. I whispered, "You got him, and you got this."

Evil radiated off of Moody. He glanced at us briefly, then stood still before those in the courtroom, an unrepentant predator stripped bare, finally facing the consequences of his actions.

After thirteen years of silence, Moody, age sixty-two, pleaded guilty to kidnapping, raping, and murdering seventeen-year-old Brittanee. In that moment, justice finally found its voice.

Moody's statement was raw and unfiltered, delivered with the weight of a confessed monster: "I was a monster. I was a monster then [referring to his previous crime in California], and I was a monster when I took Brittanee Drexel's life."

It was an admission of evil—cold, clinical, and unflinching. He continued, voice breaking: "I don't have the words to express how horrible I feel.... I'm very sorry."

The courtroom shifted. Faces softened. That sorrow, though overdue, landed like thunder. No excuse, no mitigation. Just the lifelong burden of what he had done.

Judge R. Ferrell Cothran Jr. heard statements from Brittanee's family. Dawn read, "You [Moody] will forever carry the scars of what my daughter did to you, and I hope you are haunted by what you did to her. Today, no one wins."

Dawn's voice carried not hatred but undeniable authority. A mother who refused to bend. A mother who refused to yield.

When the sentencing came, the judge gave Moody what the law demanded: life in prison with no possibility of parole. Plus an additional sixty consecutive years for kidnapping and rape.

Moody stood, degraded by his own confession, tears streaking down his face while he silently acknowledged the judge's words: "We are all products of the decisions we make in life, and I can't tell you how many times I've seen people give up their long-term happiness for immediate pleasure. And you gave up a lot of people's long-term happiness for your immediate pleasure."

He nodded. Unable to look at his victim's name on paper, yet forced to live under its weight.

In that courtroom, something irreversible was sealed. A predator who'd hidden behind decades of history and silence had been exposed, stripped of denial. He claimed remorse. He admitted guilt. But it was the sentence, a fortress of justice, that finally spoke loudest.

No one cheered. The relief was quiet—a collective exhalation that justice, although late, had been served. For Dawn and for Brittanee, it wasn't closure. It was an acknowledgment that a system, a mother, and a community had refused to let Brittanee's story end in disappearance.

That day, we bore witness to punishment and truth. And if that truth can resonate beyond those courthouse walls, then justice, typically slow, demanding, and grim, will not have been in vain.

We walked out of the courthouse to the throngs of press outside. Solicitor Richardson and Sheriff Weaver hosted a press conference. We all stood by as the press asked about the investigation, the possibility of other victims of Moody's, and if Angel Vause would face charges. Weaver and Richardson played it close to the vest and expressed appreciation to their team and ours. After the press conference, Dawn and I walked over to meet the Taylors and their pastor. Dawn embraced this family, who had been wrongly accused of being involved in Brittanee's death. They were appreciative and kind.

That was part of her healing, too. For a long period of time, her ire had been focused on the Taylors.

Our team spent the evening at the house on the bay where Dawn was staying.

The following day, we reviewed the case with Agent Connolly and his team at the FBI offices, including reports and photographs of the excavation. It was highly emotional but part of the healing process for Dawn.

There was one more person who deserved justice and still hadn't received it. Her day would come, although it would take over two more years.

CHAPTER 9

SHE'S NO ANGEL

FOLLOWING MOODY'S PLEA AND SENTENCING, Agent Connolly and his team never stopped. They knew Angel was not being honest and wanted to hold her accountable for her role. Angel was eventually federally indicted for lying to the FBI.

In July 2024, Vause, Moody's longtime girlfriend, finally pleaded guilty to multiple counts of lying to federal agents.

Her false statements had not been trivial mistakes: she'd claimed that Brittanee had accompanied them "voluntarily" to smoke drugs, feigned ignorance about Brittanee's whereabouts, and lied about who held Brittanee's phone—the only lifeline that Brittanee could have used. Each lie was a blade, cutting deeper into the truth.

Federal prosecutors didn't mince words. According to the Department of Justice, Vause "concealed the truth of what happened...for more than thirteen years," and "facilitated the kidnapping of a child." She hadn't just misled investigators. She'd obstructed justice and stolen critical time from a family begging for answers.

In February 2025, Angel Vause was sentenced to eighteen years behind bars. Eighteen years that will force her to sit alone with the truth of her betrayal. United States District Judge Richard

M. Gergel labeled Vause a "key participant in this tragedy," someone who had lured and isolated Brittanee, and then had weaponized deceit under oath.

In court, Vause offered apologies and blamed addiction. But remorse drizzles too late when measured in decades. The damage had already been done: Brittanee's phone had been silenced, the body buried, the truth buried under layers of deception. Justice in this case didn't punish just Moody's violence; it punished Vause's concealment.

Make no mistake: Vause was as guilty as Moody. She'd engineered the setup. She'd robbed a helpless teenager of escape. She'd robbed a mother of years. And she'd tried to rob Brittanee of the dignity of truth.

But on that day in February, the sentence of eighteen years in prison made one thing clear—there would be no more hiding in the shadows.

• • •

Dawn Drexel was a force. Her desperation didn't lead to surrender; it sparked a fury that refused to dim, year after year, headline after headline, until justice had no place left to hide.

Dawn was the constant. Her belief kept the case alive when everything else around it faded. She traveled across states, stared down monsters, called out cowardice, and brought more urgency to our efforts than any siren ever could. She didn't do it alone; she built an army. Not with weapons or politics, but with persistence. She pulled people into her cause, one by one, with her voice and her pain. I was proud to be one of those she brought into the fold. We became her soldiers—detectives, agents, spokespeople, and prosecutors—fighting by her side, not just for her daughter but for every parent who deserves the truth.

Brittanee Drexel mattered. Her story shook a nation. And it was her mother's fire that lit the way. Dawn proved what a single person, armed with nothing but love and resolve, could do.

In the end, justice answered her call, not because it was easy, but because she never let the world forget her daughter's name. I truly believe that if Dawn weren't as committed to finding Brittanee as she was, authorities would have eventually walked away from the case.

Dawn turned desperation into determination. This fight was about a career criminal, kidnapper, and monster versus a mother looking for her lost daughter. My money was on Dawn, and I was right.

CHAPTER 10

PIVOTING FROM PROSECUTING TO HAVING A PURPOSE

AFTER COVID, LIFE RETURNED TO normal and even a faster pace at the District Attorney's Office. I was carrying many cases and my private practice was continuing to grow. I was approaching my twenty-year anniversary as a prosecutor. On April 4, 2024, twenty years since my first day, I retired from the Luzerne County District Attorney's Office. I wasn't sure what life as a former prosecutor would feel like.

As a prosecutor and in those courtrooms, I had grown into myself through openings, closings, cross-examinations, and verdicts, in victories and losses, and in the relationships forged through the relentless pursuit of justice.

But the world was changing.

Who are we when the work stops? What remains when the title is gone? What, if anything, still calls to us?

I was grappling with those questions in real time when Brittanee Drexel's case suddenly roared back to life. A case that had haunted the headlines and hearts for over a decade. A case with layers of broken systems, a mother who refused to give up, and an ending that had long felt unreachable.

I wasn't the prosecutor in this story, but justice doesn't always wear a badge or sit behind a seal. Sometimes it speaks through experience. Sometimes it finds its next fight through a different lens.

When I first stepped into the Drexel case, not in an official capacity but as someone who had lived in the heart of that kind of battle, I didn't expect it to shake me so deeply. I didn't expect the ache in Dawn's voice to echo in my own soul.

I didn't expect the rush of urgency I felt when I looked over the case files, the interviews, the hollowed eyes of those who had searched for far too long. And I didn't expect it to make me feel as if I had found something I didn't even know I'd lost: a sense of purpose.

The Drexel case changed me. It reminded me why I'd walked into a courtroom in the first place. Not for the prestige or the verdict (although I don't mind either of those), but for the people behind the case.

Dawn Drexel was fighting for her daughter, her sanity, her family, and her truth. She was showing the world that motherhood, when wrapped around heartbreak, can become a weapon of unmatched power.

And I couldn't walk away from that. I didn't want to.

The Drexel case supercharged a passion I hadn't fully understood until that point: the desire to give a voice to the voiceless from a different seat.

As a legal analyst. As a storyteller. As someone who could take what I had seen in the trenches and translate it for the world, so these stories wouldn't be forgotten, minimized, or misunderstood.

The prosecutor title may no longer be on my letterhead, but it's still in my blood. The Drexel case reminded me that justice doesn't stop at conviction. It's also about visibility.

It's about educating the public on what really happens in the courtroom, in the interrogation room, and behind the headlines. It's about keeping the flame lit long after the cameras turn away.

That's what this case gave me. A new mission. A new identity.

I may have closed the chapter as a prosecutor, but the book of justice, the one I was always meant to write, is still wide open.

LESSONS IN MOTIVATION

Perseverance doesn't always wear armor. Sometimes, it shows up quietly—such as in the way Dawn Drexel endured not with noise but with relentless grace. Her resilience wasn't just admirable; it was instructional. The kind of strength that holds steady when everything else is broken.

Dawn didn't just hold on. She brought reinforcements. Her fight became a shared one. That's the power of community. When you believe in something so deeply, people show up to believe with you. And that belief can move things even when the system stalls.

The truth might go quiet, but it never vanishes. That's one of the most important lessons of all.

Truth has a heartbeat. It keeps pulsing, even when no one's listening, waiting for someone to pick up the rhythm again. And when that happens, when someone finally listens, justice has a chance.

Practical Steps to Stay the Course—in Law, Business, or Life

A transition can feel like standing on a cliff's edge with no clear landing. But those moments of uncertainty are often where the next mission begins. Rather than rushing to fill the silence, allow yourself to sit in it. The space might be uncomfortable, but it's where clarity begins.

Unfinished business lingers for a reason. If something continues to press on your spirit—an unresolved idea, a lost opportunity, a mission that never quite left you—consider that the door isn't closed, just waiting. Go back. The work you were meant to do might still be waiting for you.

Support doesn't always come in the form of teams and task forces. Sometimes it means showing up for someone else who refuses to give up. Be the person who stands with the determined—whether it's a grieving mother, a struggling colleague, or a dreamer on the verge of giving up. Your presence could be the tipping point that pushes everything forward.

Keep track of more than the milestones.

Capture the human moments, the ones filled with tension, fear, resolve, and breakthroughs. These moments are not just memories. They are proof of growth. They will remind you who you are when the next hard moment comes.

No matter your profession or path, remember this: technical skill will earn you trust, but heart is what will earn you respect. You can prepare endlessly, study everything, and strategize every move, but in the end, it's your integrity, your empathy, and your refusal to quit that become your signature.

Recently, a reporter asked Dawn Drexel if the sentencing of Angel Vause had finally brought her closure.

Dawn responded as only Dawn could. She looked at the reporter and said, "I don't believe in closure. I believe in resolution."

LESSONS IN MOTIVATION: A CREED FORGED IN BLOOD

Looking back, I started this journey as a young and idealistic attorney. I was not the perfect lawyer and stumbled. I have learned that there is true evil in this world, but there remains much good.

Sometimes, good people need someone to even the odds in life. Sheep don't protect sheep from the wolves; it's that simple, so to protect the herd requires a prosecutor to have the capacity for their own brand of mayhem.

These cases and many others took me to some dark places. I survived and, looking back, have learned great truths about life. The fates of the evildoers that I prosecuted were sealed when my young mother showed me there was no cavalry coming to save us. She showed me the value of love, hard work, and fighting for yourself and others. She rose above despair, sadness, and the odds.

The fates of these killers were sealed when I was given the honor of lifting my uncle Godfrey up. I channeled the pain and sadness I felt for him into helping him. I did the same for the many victims that I have served. That's the secret: don't let the pain destroy you, let it push you forward.

You don't try cases.

You fight wars.

Walk into that courtroom with your heart pounding, your suit pressed, and your soul ready to bleed if that's what justice demands.

If you're going to carry the weight of the dead, the grieving mothers, the terrified survivors—you don't do it halfway. You do it like your own life depends on the verdict.

Dress Like You Mean It

Appearance is armor.

A tailored suit. Sharp tie. Shined shoes. Not vanity—intention. You walk in looking like someone who cannot be ignored. The jury sees it. The defendant feels it. The defense resents it.

This isn't fashion—it's control. It says, "I am prepared. I am relentless."

Feel Everything: Worry, Cry, Love It

If you don't worry, you're not ready. If you don't feel sick before opening statements, you don't care enough. Let the worry sharpen you, not weaken you.

Cry, alone if you must, in your car after meeting a victim's mother, in the hallway after a bad ruling. Those tears aren't weakness. They're fuel. They remind you of why you're here.

Yes, it's okay to love this. To love the fight. To love the calling. To love standing between evil and innocent. That love is the only thing powerful enough to carry the burden.

Be Bombastic. Be Loud. Be Unafraid.

A courtroom is a battlefield, and your voice is your weapon.

Yell when truth demands it.

Whisper when pain speaks louder than rage.

Cry if it's real, if it's earned, if it confronts injustice with raw humanity.

Smile, let everyone know you are at peace in the chaos.

Jurors don't remember perfect speeches. They remember how you made them feel.

Name the Darkness and Walk Through It

"I've taken on defendants with street names such as "Ruthless," "Hazard," and "Monster."

Murderers. Predators. The kind who smirks through testimony. Name them. Confront them. Break the myth of their fear. Some need to be called by name, like "Hugo," not to raise their status, but to let them know you see them, aren't afraid, and know who they are.

You are not there to negotiate with evil. You are there to drag it into the light and show the jury exactly what it did.

See It as War—Fight to Win

Every witness is a soldier. Every exhibit is a bullet. Every closing word is a final charge.

You aren't trying a case—you're staging a final stand. Don't apologize for wanting to win. For wanting justice like breath in your chest. For wanting a verdict that echoes through the victim's cemetery stones.

Carry the Mother with You

Every case has a mother. A family. A hole that will never close.

Let their faces wake you up at night. Let their voices haunt you. Let their grief burn inside you so that when you stand to speak, you speak not for yourself—but for those who can't.

Epilogue

IN MAY 2025, NICOLE AND I celebrated our twentieth wedding anniversary. We had always wanted to travel to Italy, but there was never a time that wasn't crazy busy in our lives—and the kids were small.

This year, I said, "No excuses—we're going."

Well, Pope Francis passed away on April 21, and a papal conclave began just over a week before we were set to leave.

On May 8, the College of Cardinals named Pope Leo XIV, an American, head of the Catholic Church. It was one week before we were scheduled to tour the Vatican.

I loved Italy and felt very much at home there. We first stayed in an apartment in Sorrento. Then we were planning to travel to Rome via a train out of Naples on May 17.

We arranged for Filippo, our driver for the week, to pick us up and drive us to the station. He was a seventy-year-old Sorrento native and unintentionally hilarious. He made us repeatedly promise to be ready promptly at 6:05 a.m. to catch the 8 a.m. train out of Naples for Rome.

We met Filippo early and headed out.

We drove through the cobblestone streets of Sorrento, and I could tell something was wrong. Filippo said, "We have a flat tire." We pulled over. He called someone on his phone and spoke in Italian. He was clearly directing someone to meet him.

Within minutes, we pulled into a gas station, and a young man in another van arrived immediately to assist. We had built in enough time that we shouldn't be late.

I was anxious, though, because if we didn't get to Rome that particular day, we'd have a hard time getting there. Pope Leo's inaugural mass was set for the following day. US vice president J.D. Vance and Ukrainian president Volodymyr Zelensky were going to be in attendance. Things were going to be busy at the Vatican.

The young man placed the spare tire on quickly, and we were on our way. Filippo and the man were conversing in Italian excitedly. As we left, I asked Filippo, "Who was that man?"

He said, "My son-in-law."

As we traveled on the highway toward Naples, I could hear a thumping on the other side of the van. Then I smelled burning rubber. I said, "Filippo, I think the van is on fire."

"Oh, Madonna," Filippo said. We had another flat.

I started to wonder if God was trying to tell us something.

Filippo pulled over on the side of the highway. He ran into oncoming traffic, trying to flag down another van with his arms flailing to take us to the train. I thought he was going to be killed.

He managed to stop a driver passing by and quickly loaded us into the stranger's van. In a foreign country. He said something to the driver in Italian and waved us into the van.

We made it to the train—and to Rome, and into the Vatican.

I was excited as we approached St. Peter's Square. I was absolutely mesmerized by the beauty and magnificence of this place. There were throngs of people, and the staff was setting up for the next day's papal inaugural mass.

As we approached the entryway, I stood under the balcony where just over a week ago the world had seen Pope Leo step out for the first time.

As we entered, Michelangelo's *Pietà*—a sculpture of Mary holding her broken son, Jesus—greeted us.

I stood there in awe. I'm not religious, but I consider myself a spiritual person.

The *Pietà* rattled me. Mary was holding Jesus as if he were a baby, as she had when he was born in a stable more than thirty years earlier.

I had seen images of the *Pietà* in my years in Catholic school, and recreations in many churches. But standing before the actual sculpture was completely different. Michelangelo had managed to capture the hollowness, the deep sadness, on Mary's face.

Her eyes showed rage, heartache, guilt, pain, confusion, helplessness, hopelessness.

I knew that look. I'd seen it many times before—the look not only of a mother who'd outlived her child, but of the mother of a murdered child.

It reminded me of the resilience of so many mothers I'd encountered along the way.

I was in the process of writing this book, and fate had brought me to this amazing testament of a mother's strength.

Writing this book and looking back over the past two decades have been therapeutic.

I didn't want to write just another prosecutor's book—beating my chest and bragging about courtroom triumphs. I was scared during many of the moments recounted. I was afraid that I was going too far. That my skills weren't up to par.

But I pushed forward—because of who I was fighting for and what I was fighting against.

These cases and the many others did some damage to me and left some scars, but they were all worth it.

My hope is that you, the reader, who may be engaged in your own fight—in a courtroom, in a job, in your family, or in your life—can find strength in the stories that I've shared. That you can find hope and light in the darkest places.

This book is a homage to my mother; to Nicole, an amazing mother to our children; to the moms I fought for; to the colleagues I stood with; and to everyone along the way who taught me a little lesson that I brought into those courtrooms.

So much of our society today is focused on money. How big is your house? What kind of car do you drive?

I certainly like those things. But the greatest victories I've ever been a part of have had nothing to do with money. They've had everything to do with making a wrong right. I'm still very much that boy who practiced Al Pacino monologues in the mirror, and I still get choked up watching *Rocky* movies. Find that hope inside of yourself. Find that reason to fight.

Find that discipline wrapped in a task that inspires you—and become part of a story that is bigger than yourself.

I wasn't stronger, faster, smarter, or richer than anyone else. I had no special skills—other than believing in myself.

My advice to everyone out there is this:

Lead with your heart. Let that be your compass and your motivation. The rest of you—including your mind and an unexpected work ethic—will follow.

Many times in life, I've had to be the hard-ass and the tough guy. But just as many times, I've had to be a shoulder for someone to cry on and an ear to listen to someone.

I stand on the shoulders of the colleagues who stood with me in those courtrooms—and of my family, who stood behind me when I was distracted or caught up in some battle.

Their love and support made everything possible.

Thank you, Mom. I love you.

Acknowledgments

To Nicole, my beautiful wife—you are an amazing partner and mother. Thank you for always standing by my side and for the incredible life we have built.

To my children, Dominick and Victoria, who shared Daddy with the bad guys and girls for far too many years.

Dominick, my son—you inspire me. You are a better man than I am: kinder, smarter, and taller. And I am so proud of you.

Victoria, my baby—in you I see the passion to fight for others and the ability to deliver, but I also see Mommy's goodness. I cannot wait to see the journey that awaits you.

To my two late fathers, Gary Ferentino and Charles Grimes—thank you for being wonderful husbands to my mother and incredible fathers to me.

To my brother Maurice "Moe," the trailblazer—thank you for being fearless and for always being yourself.

To my brother Jude "JuJu," my confidant and my rock—your love, instincts, and humor mean the world to me.

To my brother Jason "Jay," my twin—from literally day one, you have been by my side. You are an amazing dad and a success in every way. I was never alone. And of course, thank you to Tiffany

"TT," your wonderful wife and an incredible mother, for taking you off my hands.

To my in-laws, Jack and Donna Linskey—thank you for your support through the years of having a son-in-law who was often distracted, for your love, your help, your humor, and for the greatest gift of all: Nicole.

To Drs. Christopher and Jeannette Sanders, my brilliant brother and sister-in-law—I am in awe of your accomplishments and the parents you have become.

To my nieces and nephews—Anthony "AJ," Marah, Paulie, Michael, Jude "Baby Jude," and Angelina "Gigi" Ferentino, and Jack and Reed Sanders—Uncle Jarrett loves all of you very much.

To my godparents, Tony and Rose Martorana, who have always been a shining example of love and hard work.

To my law partners and friends—Charles Shaffer, Paul Pugliese, William Finnegan, Shannon Crake Lapsansky, and Rachel Finnegan—thank you for tolerating me as a partner and for serving our profession with distinction and honor.

To Michael "Deuce" Lombardo—thank you for choosing to be my brother and for always being there.

To Mr. Michael Lombardo, who told me when I was fifteen years old that I was going to be a lawyer—you knew before I did, and I came to believe you. Thank you for your guidance and teachings throughout my life.

To my friend Dave Pedri—you always have my back, and I hope you know I will always have yours. Thank you for always letting me think out loud with you.

To Jason Valenti, my lifelong friend and true crime partner—I treasure your friendship, your confidence in me, your incredible sense of humor, and your technical savvy.

To Ronnie Lieback—thank you for your friendship and support throughout the telling of my story. And thank you to Pam and Enzo for generously sharing you while we worked. We did it.

To Steph Watts—thank you for your friendship, compassion for the stories you tell, and commitment to your work.

To Sergeant Michelle Wood-Garcia of the Chicago Police Department—thank you for your counsel, talent, and friendship.

To my friend Lauren Conlin—your passion and confidence are contagious.

To the judges, district attorneys, assistant district attorneys, and public defenders of Luzerne County—despite the battles and the headlines, it was an honor and privilege to work alongside you. Each of you serves our community with dignity and honor.

To Judge David Lupas—thank you for bringing me into your district attorney's office and for your example of calm and professionalism.

To Jackie Musto Carroll—thank you for your friendship and faith in me during your time as district attorney and beyond.

To Judge Stefanie Salavantis—thank you for the trust we built and for the grace with which you led the district attorney's office.

To District Attorney Sam Sanguedolce—from our years at St. Mary's to the wild journey we took together, thank you for your leadership and friendship.

To retired Trooper Gerald Sachney—thank you for your dogged determination and humility.

To the late Detective Lt. R. Gary "Cap" Capitano—I miss you every day and will never forget you.

To Mamie Phillips—the toughest prosecutor I have ever met and my friend.

To Michelle Giza, an unsung hero of the Luzerne County District Attorney's Office, for your dedication and hard work.

To the members of law enforcement, I have had the pleasure to represent and stand with, especially my many friends in the Pennsylvania State Police—the honor, privilege, and pleasure were all mine.

To Sylvester Stallone—Thank you for creating *Rocky*. You showed the world to never underestimate a short Italian from Pennsylvania with heart and self-belief.

To Al Pacino—thank you for giving a kid with little confidence a body of work to practice in the mirror and to help shape my own brand of drama.

To Dr. Wayne W. Dyer—thank you for your teachings, your writing, and your inspiration.